Raising a Father

Raising a Father

ARJUN SEN

iUniverse, Inc.
New York   Bloomington

iUniverse books may be ordered through booksellers or by contacting:

iUniverse
1663 Liberty Drive
Bloomington, IN 47403
www.iuniverse.com
1-800-Authors (1-800-288-4677)

Because of the dynamic nature of the Internet, any Web addresses or links contained in this book may have changed since publication and may no longer be valid. The views expressed in this work are solely those of the author and do not necessarily reflect the views of the publisher, and the publisher hereby disclaims any responsibility for them.

ISBN: 978-1-4401-5803-2 (sc)
ISBN: 978-1-4401-5802-5 (ebook)
ISBN: 978-1-4401-5801-8 (dj)

Printed in the United States of America

iUniverse rev. date: 10/19/2009

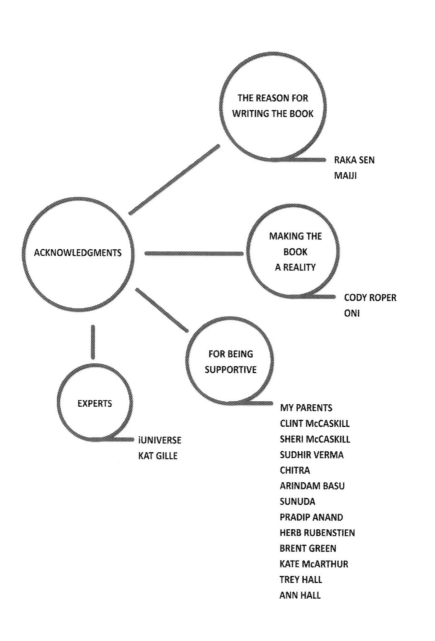

THE REASON FOR
WRITING THE BOOK

RAKA SEN
MAIJI

ACKNOWLEDGMENTS

MAKING THE
BOOK
A REALITY

CODY ROPER
ONI

FOR BEING
SUPPORTIVE

EXPERTS

iUNIVERSE
KAT GILLE

MY PARENTS
CLINT McCASKILL
SHERI McCASKILL
SUDHIR VERMA
CHITRA
ARINDAM BASU
SUNUDA
PRADIP ANAND
HERB RUBENSTIEN
BRENT GREEN
KATE McARTHUR
TREY HALL
ANN HALL

PREFACE

During my days in the corporate world, some wise, rapid-corporate-stair-climbing friend once told me, "Arjun, in order to achieve bigger glories, one must make smaller sacrifices in life." I know he was referring to spending less time with family, not being there for one's children's special moments, and similar "small" sacrifices in one's personal life. Learning from him, I always thought that I needed to make personal sacrifices to make it big in the corporate world. I really wish now that I could reach out and find that corporate-stair-climbing friend. I want to tell him three things.

First, my friend, you can have both. You do not have to sacrifice personal life to reach professional success. It is true that I do not have the corner office in the Taj Mahal of corporate buildings. Building and maintaining my consulting business by working from home is not easy. Things like getting health insurance as an individual are especially tough. On the other hand, I have a one-minute commute to work, my work life automatically pauses when I get a call from my daughter, and my team and I work on some fun projects. Not bad to have the best of both worlds.

Second, I measure success differently today. Even as our small consulting company is being shaken to the core because of the financial turmoil in the world, I know I somehow have to survive the next two years. Raka will leave for college in two years, and I believe my success will be determined by the time I can spend with her.

Third, you were right. Yes, at times, in order to achieve bigger glories, one must make smaller sacrifices in life. But you got the glories reversed. The smaller sacrifice is the professional sacrifice. If you lose a job you will find another one, but if you lose your connection with your family, will you ever find it again? I have learned to take this job seriously. It is a job from which I cannot take even a day off. I have learned not to close doors for my daughter but instead to inspire her to dream big and act on achieving her dreams. I have learned to be there to experience every moment. I have learned to listen to her.

This is a story of my daughter, Raka, evolving in life. It is important to know that I have an important role in this story. As Bill Cosby would say, yes, "I was instrumental in bringing her to the world." And yet it will not take a rocket scientist to figure out that I have had more than my fair share of failures in life. But all through every failure in my life, there has been one thread of saving grace: every day I have tried to be a good dad to my daughter as I have watched her blossom into a wonderful young woman. *Tried* is the key word here.

Fortunately, this is not a story about me trying to be a good dad. Instead, it is a story about how a little girl used all her charm, her patience, her love, and her caring nature to train her dad. She trained me to be a better dad and, more importantly, a better person.

The story of my daughter is based on real events in our lives. But reality is relative. During my divorce I learned a hard truth from Raka: for her there was *her dad's reality*, *her mother's reality*, and then *her own reality*. The only thing that mattered to her was her own reality, but it also confused her that all three realities did not always sync with each other.

In this story, I try to stay as close as I can to Raka's reality and my reality. If you were a witness to our lives, you may see some of the events a little differently. It could be that in my attempt to glorify the story I have painted the events with a few magic colors from a proud dad. I feel that doing so is not harmful. After all, it is not every day I get a chance to costar in a story with the most wonderful person on this planet.

WAKE UP! WAKE UP! THE DAY AFTER 9/11 LOUISVILLE, KENTUCKY, 2001

My life thus far has been full of wake-up calls. Some of the wake-up calls have been figurative, some have been literal. Some have been loud, some have been prolonged. There have been times I have woken up after a wake-up call, and there have been times I have snoozed. Every wake-up call in my life, figurative or literal, has had a purpose, and it has always been up to me to figure that purpose out. This is the story of the biggest wake-up call in my life, which happened the day after 9/11.

All of us remember where we were during the horrors of 9/11. Even today I cannot comprehend the full magnitude of the horror. It was like watching the scariest movie on this planet and then being told that it was real; it shocked the entire existence out of most of us. I was in Louisville, Kentucky. Some of my coworkers were coming back from a trip to Toronto. The cell phones were down, and none of us knew how our coworkers were going to make it back home. The same day, at the same time in the morning, my brother was flying on an American Airlines flight from London to Chicago. At the time of the horrifying events, his plane must have been just a few hundred miles east of New York City. Fortunately his flight got rerouted to Goose Bay, Canada.

The world was in shock; my life was filled with uncertainty. But even with all this turmoil, I was still not ready for what happened the next morning.

The day after 9/11, everyone at my company took a forced vacation day. With travel restricted, there were no meetings. I was at home, alternating between watching the news on TV and the news on the Internet.

In the middle of this anxious time, Raka came and sat next to me. She rested her head on my shoulder and asked, "What are you doing, Dad?" It was one of those casual discussions where she would ask me something and I would answer her without looking up from my laptop. Usually we would have a conversation while I checked my e-mail—I was a master at multitasking. But that day's conversation was very different, and I was not ready for what was going to hit me. The random questions and talking continued, and then there was silence. I turned and stared at my eight-year-old daughter and realized that she was staring back at me.

I was uncomfortable with the silence. I had to ask something. Just as I would with any of my employees, I asked Raka, "How are we doing?" It is such a strange question. It is a setup. Employees always answered the question with, "Good," and that would lift the burden off me. If we were doing well, then there was nothing to worry about. With employees, I would follow up and have a meaningless, superficial conversation, then look at my assistant outside to indicate that time was up.

But with Raka, I was in for a big surprise. She looked at me and said, "Not good at all." I thought I had heard something wrong. I asked her again, but the answer was the same, only this time it was more determined.

I was in unfamiliar territory. I was not prepared at all. I asked her immediately, "Are you not feeling well? What is wrong?"

She looked at me again and said, "Nothing, Dad." She gently cuddled up next to me. I closed my laptop and put the TV on mute and then pulled Raka close to me. She looked up and smiled.

I asked her again, "What is wrong, baby?"

She sighed, looked at me, and said, "You don't know me, Dad."

I failed to understand the pain she felt as she made this statement.

I felt challenged. Instead of trying to understand why she felt this way, I got defensive. "Of course I know you," I replied. I wished she would believe me just because I *felt* I knew her.

Raka thought for a while and then got out a piece of paper. She scribbled something on it and gave it to me. She had written three questions. The questions were simple, and I was sure I could handle them. But I still could not believe what was happening: I was getting a surprise quiz. The three questions were:

1. Who is my best friend?
2. What is my favorite restaurant?
3. What is the best thing you and I have ever done?

As I tackled the first question, I made a mental list of all her friends. Through a methodical process of elimination I came up with two names, and bingo! The answer flashed in front of my eyes. I had done this so many times in the business world—eliminated low-probability options to come up with the answer that had the highest probability of success. This was a fun game. I thought we should play it more often. I could get good at this.

I disclosed my answer with a chuckle, but my smile died instantly when Raka immediately said, "nope!" What came after that was even worse. "Look, I told you, you don't know me."

Unwilling to admit defeat, I realized I could still get two out of three answers right. The other two questions were easier. I decided to keep the restaurant question for last, since my career was in restaurant marketing. There was no way I would get that one wrong. So I focused on our favorite things we'd done. There were so many to choose from. Was it the time I took her to Churchill Downs for the races? Was it the time I took her ice skating? Was it our Hawaii trip? Was it the time she came to work with me? Or was it the time when I bought her that new dress from Macy's New York City? So many special moments; of course I knew her.

Finally I settled with the ice-skating trip. She loves to skate. It had to be one of the best. Raka listened but did not comment. Then she asked me, "And what is my favorite restaurant?" Of course it was Papa John's pizza. I worked there, and Raka had even met the founder, John. That was easy. I delivered my answer and awaited the hug from her to confirm that I knew her. Nailing the final two answers would give me a face-saving win.

Raka looked very puzzled. What followed was the worst performance appraisal I have ever received. It was brutal. And I cannot argue that I did not deserve it.

"Dad, do you remember what we did when we went ice skating? You took me there after canceling twice. I was all dressed and ready to go both the times you canceled. The one time we were actually there, you took a table close to the rink to see me. Every time I came around you waved at me, but you were on your cell phone the entire time. Then you came up and told me it was time to leave. We had some popcorn and left. It was fun, Dad, but you were not there."

I was confused. What was Raka talking about? I had been there. I had canceled a meeting with my boss to be there.

Raka went on. "My favorite time with you is when you pick me up from school, we hold hands, we stop at an ice cream place, we talk, and then we go home and I sit on the couch next to you and we watch the *Bill Cosby Show*."

Now I was really confused. What was she talking about? She did not like the big, grand things we did? She liked the day-to-day activities more? Very strange, yet very interesting. I have to admit that I had had no clue.

"Now, about my favorite restaurant. It's Applebee's. Every time I go there they give me a free balloon, and I love their mac-n-cheese the best." She paused. "Look, Dad, you do not know me." That was followed with a long, deep sigh.

I was disheartened. If this had been a performance appraisal at a job, the next thing I heard would have been, "You're fired." I realized I needed to use my best skills to get out of this jam. At work, I had two strategies that would get me out of any crisis: either I deferred the problem so I had more time to solve it or I switched the subject to a different topic in which I had a better chance of succeeding. I wanted to make a comeback with my daughter, so I was ready to use both my tactics. I told her, "Raka, I know you do not like Louisville, Kentucky. I know you want to go back to Denver. I am trying to get us back there. I promise it will happen soon. Give me a little time, baby, okay?"

Raka had a determined look on her face. She was not going to let me sway her. She told me, "Dad, I love you, so you do not have to lie to me. I want to go to Denver—you know that—but if you really wanted to go to Denver, by now we would have gone back."

It felt like my little girl had taken a dagger and punched it into my heart. I was shattered. There are no other words to describe that experience. I tried to explain the lack of career opportunities in Denver for professionals at my level and other market factors, but honestly, I did not know what I was saying. As I spoke, Raka's words echoed in my mind over and over: "Dad, you do not have to lie to me." I was nearly in tears.

Raka would not let me off easily. She persisted, "If you are trying, how many interviews have you had in Denver? Why did you go to Detroit to interview the other day?"

The message had been delivered. It had been delivered loud and clear. I could see my future life. I would be sixty-five, have tons of money in the bank, and be retired from a very celebrated career. I would have made it onto numerous who's-who lists, but my life would be about counting days. I would count the days until two annual phone calls from my daughter. One would come on Father's Day, and one would come on my birthday. They would be brief calls in which she wished me happy birthday, I asked her how she was, and she said "Good," and then there would be a pause. She would say, "Dad, please take care of yourself," and hang up. I could hear the sound of the disconnected phone call. It echoed in my ears.

I wanted to ask her questions, but what would I ask her? I did not know her. I sat and cried. *How did I get here?* I wondered. *Why did I not see this coming?*

As I thought more that evening, I realized this was the biggest and loudest wake-up call in my life. The reality made me want to pull the sheets over my head and go back to sleep, but a small part of me wanted to wake up and change my life.

~ Some wake-up calls we really wish we had not heard. Waking up forces us to accept reality. ~

GROWING UP IN INDIA

THE LEGEND OF MAIJI
KOLKATA, INDIA, 1950S

Maiji, Bina Sen, was my paternal grandmother. After a brilliant academic life, Maiji settled down and married my grandfather. Soon they had four children, my father being the second of the four. Maiji was an accomplished singer and sang next to India's poet laureate, Rabindranath Tagore.

Everything was going perfectly in Maiji's dream life till she turned forty and my grandfather passed away. The next year, Maiji lost her youngest child, my dad's youngest sister.

Maiji was living in India in the 1950s. It was a tough time for a single woman with three kids to enter the workforce, but she never looked back. Soon she was working for an insurance company, and after long days of hard work she came home to tend to her three children.

Maiji's accomplishments can be summarized by the fact that she put her three kids through college: my aunt through medical school and my father and uncle through engineering school. On top of this, Maiji built her dream home in Kolkata, India. In those days there were no consumer loans, so everything Maiji built was paid for as she moved forward, adding room by room. The house is a tribute to Maiji's dream. It is an engineering marvel because she built it one room at a time, a very unique concept. When I think about Maiji's accomplishment, the only thing I can compare it to is the effort of an ant. An ant is known for being able to carry nearly ten times its weight. But Maiji far surpassed that with her monumental efforts.

When I was young, Maiji had already retired. When I think about my early days, most of my memories are connected with my Maiji. During those days, she was the one person who stood at the helm of my life to guide it in the right direction. As I started writing this book, I realized that Maiji was the Yoda in my life. She laid the groundwork for my future. It is true that Raka will unlock many of my capabilities in the future, but I feel the future would not have happened without Maiji's groundwork.

~ Some actions go beyond days and months to affect others. Maiji's actions did just that. ~

WAKE UP! WAKE UP! KOLKATA, INDIA, 1972

This is the story of a series of daily wake-up calls from Maiji that continued every day, without fail, for twelve years.

Maiji's commitment to my education was unparalleled. She must have figured out early on that I was not the smartest of all kids, and hence working hard was the only way I would be able to accomplish something in life. She would remind me over and over that in life, success comes from "99 percent perspiration and 1 percent inspiration." I heard that many times.

Maiji's bedroom was next to the room in which my brother, Oni, and I used to sleep. At four o'clock every morning, Maiji would scream my name from her bed. I had five minutes to wake up, and if I did not wake up on my own, Maiji would come in and shake me up. I always preferred to wake up before she came in.

It was not over after I woke up. I would go to the bathroom to brush my teeth and freshen up, and Maiji would keep track of time. If I was in the bathroom for more than five minutes, I would get my second call. I was conditioned to run out of the bathroom when the call came in.

So now I was awake, I was up, and I was all freshened up. I would sit at my desk to study. At 4:30 AM, Maiji would get up and make hot cocoa for me, which she served me at my desk. There were times I dozed off at my desk—and that was the worst thing I could do. If

Maiji caught me dozing, she would grab me by the back of my head and shove my face against the table. My chin banging on the table was a rude wake-up call, as intense as it gets.

Now when I think back, some of Maiji's tactics are bound to raise eyebrows. I am amazed, though, when I think back on her wake-up calls, at how consistent they were, every morning, every day, for twelve years. Yes, there were times Maiji would assume a scary, non-characteristic, somewhat cruel role, but today I look above all that. I see a visionary who was building a habit in me; she was investing in my future. I recognize Maiji's commitment and dedication as one of the key drivers of my academic and professional success in later life.

~ The pain of today is the investment of tomorrow. There are no shortcuts to success. ~

A RELIGIOUS DISCOVERY
KOLKATA, INDIA, 1973

I was born a Hindu. We had a small worship room in the house. I did not practice organized religion, in the sense that there was no routine for me to regularly go to the temple, but my parents and Maiji both taught me to remember God every chance I could. Maiji would meditate in the morning and in the evening. My dad would start every day with a quick prayer. My brother and I were encouraged to say a quick prayer before we went to bed and before meals. On special occasions we would all go to the temple, and during the big Hindu festivals we would go wearing new clothes.

As I grew up, I realized that some of my friends were Muslims, some were Christians, and some were Buddhists. India celebrates every religion, and school was off for all religious holidays. We had days off for Hindu puja (religious) celebrations and for Christian and Islam religious festivities. Over time each religion's claim to be the "only path" confused me. I would go to the home of an Islamic friend and read signs on the walls that read, "Islam is the only way." I attended a Jesuit school, where I recited the prayer, "Our father, who art in heaven." Some of my Christian friends talked about church and prayers. My Buddhist friend was a vegetarian, as that lifestyle was directed by his religion. On top of everything else I was taking a class called Moral Science, and I was not doing too well in that class.

One evening I shared my confusion and predicament with Maiji.

Maiji responded by asking me what my religion was. I was not prepared for her trick question. I thought my religion was Hinduism, but Maiji said, "Hinduism is not a religion but a way of life." She even went on to explain, "Because Hinduism is not a religion, one cannot be converted into it. Instead, one can only adopt the Hindu way of life."

I was surprised. Maiji looked ready for a bigger discussion, but she stopped. She put her glasses on and looked through her book collection. Soon she came back with a set of books she wanted me to read. She had a translation of the Holy Koran, the New Testament, *Life and Teachings of Buddha,* and the Bhagavad Gita. She gave me a few weeks to read them.

Every day she followed up with me to make sure I was reading the books. In a month I was done, and we sat on the verandah and Maiji explained to me the concept of religions. I sat at Maiji's feet and listened in amazement. She explained that none of the religions were wrong and that every path made sense. Then she elaborated on the subject with the famous lines from Swami Vivekananda: "*Jotto moth toto poth*," which translates to, "As many faiths, that many paths." Maiji told me that there were numerous paths in life that lead to the same lake. Depending on who and where you were, you chose a path in life called your religion. Yes, your path, if lived properly, would lead you to the lake, but all the other paths would do the same.

Finally she explained that following a religion was not good enough. It was not the path that mattered: a good person lived the concept of his or her religion, not just the performed rituals. In the end, he or she would make the world a better place. At the same time, Maiji gave me examples of bad people from different religions, showing me that following a religion did not stop bad people from doing bad things.

In those four weeks, I learned more than a lifetime of lessons. I learned that I had no religion, but that I had a commitment to a lifestyle. I also was inspired to be a better person because I learned that we could all make the world better, one person at a time.

~ The world needs good people and good deeds. Religion is just a path that helps us get there. ~

SOCCER FAILURE
KOLKATA, INDIA, 1973

I was born to be a soccer star. Soccer was in my blood. As I grew up, there was not a single day that passed when I did not play soccer. I did not have the skills of a Brazilian soccer superstar, but that was not as important as my unparalleled passion for the sport.

In 1973, I was in grade three. Intraschool soccer was big, and a competitive spirit buzzed in the air. Players competed for specific positions on the teams, and I chose to try for the position of goal keeper. I was the only one interested in that position, so I got selected for my class's soccer team.

My team's first match was after school on a Friday. My parents came to watch my first game, and I was excited. The game started uneventfully for me. For the first thirty minutes, I just walked left and right anticipating a ball that never came to me. But right before halftime, my team screamed my name. I saw the ball, kicked right at me from center field. My first-ever soccer save was seconds away. It was a high kick. I looked at the ball and positioned myself in its path. I was all set. Then I decided to run forward and grab the ball as it bounced. I was at the right place when the ball bounced, but before I could grab it, it skidded on the wet field and went past me toward the goal. I saw the ball go past me in slow motion. I tried to turn and stop the ball. I begged the ball the come back to my hands. But the determined ball continued to march forward into the goal. As I watched it slowly and surely enter the goal, I saw my parents sitting just behind the goal, the perfect place to watch.

Life came out of slow motion as the ball entered the goal while my teammates desperately screamed my name. The ball stopped after crossing the goal line, and I slowly went to gather it and send it back for the game to resume. From the corner of my eye I looked at my parents. I was hoping against hope that they had not seen the goal. But they had.

Once I had retrieved the ball, I tried to kick it to the center of the field—I was angry at the ball. But it was not my day. I slipped as I was trying to kick it and fell flat on my back. The ball bounced in front of me. The captain of my team ran back, got the ball, and relieved me from my misery.

Soccer had not started well for me, but I gathered my wits and managed to grab the ball early in nearly all future goal attempts that day. Not all, but nearly all. A few minutes before the end of the match, another long ball came toward me. This time there was no scream from my teammates. There was pin-drop silence as everyone, again, looked at me. I was ready, and I was determined. I aligned myself and did not make the same mistake as before. I did not charge toward the ball but instead stood with my arms raised, ready to grab it. It bounced in front of me. I was ready. My arms were ready. I could see the ball coming to me. The ball was there, and I jumped up to grab it. But my effort fell short, and the ball went over my outreached hands and into the goal. Now my humiliation was complete. I had let my team down. As I walked back to fetch the ball, I looked at my parents with tears rolling down my cheeks. I was ready to go home.

After that day, many a time I replayed the moments in my mind. I imagined jumping up and either grabbing the ball or fisting it over the goalpost. I felt an amazing need to change the past and change that particular memory.

After that day, even though I never played goalie again, I got better at soccer. I made the school soccer team, but I have to admit I was mediocre at best. I tried hard and played hard to compensate for my lack of real soccer skills, but anytime I was alone at the soccer field, I would see little Arjun as a goalie, under the goalpost, reaching up to catch the ball—and missing.

~ We allow some failures to define us. ~

NO ART FOR YOU
KOLKATA, INDIA, 1975

Some memories are too painful to remember, but worse are the memories that are so painful that they change the path of your life forever. Those are memories you cannot simply forget, even if you wish to.

One such memory stemmed from my desire to draw and paint. As an eleven-year-old in grade five, I used to take up art projects at home whenever I got a chance. I do not think I was any good at it, but I loved colors. My brother, Oni, though, was truly talented. He could draw and sketch whatever he wanted, and what he drew actually looked like what he was planning to draw. I, on the other hand, was an accidental artist. I would play with colors and *then* look to see what I had drawn.

There might have been a career for an accidental artist like me, or so I thought until Maiji decided to take Oni and me to an art class. I remember the first day. The teacher gave Oni and me both an open invitation to draw something. Based on our accomplishments, he would assign us to different levels of classes.

I was excited. Never in my whole life had I had all the colors in the world at my disposal. I began sketching on the watercolor paper and decided to paint the sky basking in the glory of the setting sun. I loved sunsets. I drew a simple landscape of the mountains, the clouds, the river, the grasslands, the houses, and the trees. Then I focused on the sky. I was ready for my favorite sunset. I painted the sky red. In fact I poured some red paint on the paper and splashed it all over—the red sunset had taken over the whole scene. I was very proud of my work. For once I had done what I had set out to do.

My happiness and pride were short-lived. The teacher came behind me and asked me what I was doing, and before I could explain, he took my artwork away, rolled it into a ball, and trashed it. He gave me a new piece of paper and told me that "Sky cannot be red."

I had a chance for a redo. The Picasso in me was on a roll. I painted like a man possessed. This time I knew exactly what I was doing and where my fingers were going. I was doing a more authentic sunset painting. This time the last rays of the sun covered every aspect of the world. The world was red.

The teacher looked at my work and nodded his head. That day when Maiji came to pick me up, the teacher took Maiji aside and told her that my family was wasting their money in sending me to art school. I could not believe what I had just heard. Wasting money on me? The little artist's colorful world was converted into a simple black-and-white door. I was ready to leave the world of color behind. I slowly staggered my way out. As I left, I heard all the kids in the classroom behind me, but I did not dare turn and look back because my destiny and fate were already written.

I did not draw again for twenty-two years. Not once. Finally, when I was thirty-three years old and going through tough times in life, I picked up the paint again. I again became obsessed with my artwork. I loved color. I painted like a man possessed. I was trying to regain my art days. But even with the revisit, I will never try to paint the sky red. That art teacher and just one moment of his harsh judgment stole my red sky from me forever.

~ As my door was being closed, I wish someone had put his foot in to stop it. I needed that. ~

A VISIT TO THE UROLOGIST KOLKATA, INDIA, 1978

It was 1978. I was in grade eight. My life was busy as always with school, soccer, tutors, and cricket and was as hectic as it could be. I had noticed a growth on one of the fingers on my right hand, and one morning I realized that the growth was getting bigger and that it was starting to affect my writing. I was at a loss, and with Maiji out of town, things were even tougher.

That evening, a friend of my dad's came over for an evening drink. He was a renowned urologist and a surgeon. Because my dad trusted this surgeon's medical knowledge, he asked me to show him my finger. I obliged. This doctor, after reviewing my finger, exclaimed that it needed surgery. In three days, I was in his office to get my finger operation. It was not painful. I remember the pinch of the first anesthetic shot, and then I stared away from my finger as the surgery began. I could feel some mild sensations at the area. The surgery lasted a maximum of three to five minutes, and when it was done, the doctor put a bandage on my finger, patted me on the back, and walked me out. He gave me some routine advice on taking it easy for the next few days, and then he hailed a cab and paid the fare for it to take me home.

A few days later, I was back at his office for a post-surgical review. After routine chit-chat, the surgeon removed the bandage. There were three major growths, all huge, ugly, and obnoxious. It was one of the ugliest sights I've ever seen. I did not know what to do, but the surgeon seemed to know exactly what needed to be done. I remember the look in his eyes: he saw a major war ahead.

A follow-up surgery date was scheduled. By now, I knew the routine. I was all ready for "removal of the killer growths, part two." This time the surgery was longer. When I started getting a little sensation back in my fingers and thought that surgery should soon be over, I saw more intensity in the eyes of the surgeon that indicated to me that there was no immediate end in sight. Finally, the surgery was over, and, just like last time, the surgeon walked me to a cab, paid my cab fare, and sent me home.

A few days later, I decided to open the bandage. I was startled, as there was not one, not three, but a total of seven small growths fighting with each other for space on my finger. It was now the ghastliest sight on this planet. I did not want to go back to the surgeon since I knew his method of destroying these growths would mean a bigger war. I sincerely worried that any more surgery and my finger could be a casualty of friendly fire. The next few days I hid my finger under strategically placed Band-Aids.

All this time Maiji was in New Delhi. I was quite relieved when she finally returned, and I rushed to tell her about my predicament. She was calm as ever, even though she was not a doctor, as she looked closely at the mushroomlike creatures growing on my finger. Then in her calm, collected voice, she gently asked me, "Why did you visit a urologist for a finger growth? Is this what I have taught you over the years?" I realized it was kind of stupid to see a urologist for a finger growth. Maiji then went on to say, "You know you could have lost your finger."

My brother, Oni, who was witnessing this amusing conversation, decided to join in with his smart comments. "Maiji, do not be too hard on him. He went to show his finger to the urologist and risked only his finger. He might be a urologist, but think what would have happened if Arjun had gone to get his …" Maiji took one look at Oni, and Oni left the room without finishing the sentence.

Maiji started thinking and looked at my finger again. The next day, she came back from the store with some homeopathic medication and applied it to the growths. It burned a lot, but within a few days I witnessed a miracle as the growths simply vanished. I was left with only the nasty scars from the surgeries on my finger. The scars still remind me of my brother's shocking comment and Maiji's calmness in my moment of crisis. She never panicked, and she always made sure I got the treatment I needed.

~ Every problem has a simple solution. Finding it is the key. ~

SOCCER WIN
KOLKATA, INDIA, 1980

As I grew up, I played soccer at every chance I got, at school and in my neighborhood. It was in the neighborhood, where we played "six-on-six soccer," that I truly realized my fullest potential.

The year 1980 was the big year. I was on a roll as a striker on my soccer team. I had scored a goal in each of our team's matches and was leading the goal scorers' list. My team was headed to the club championship game, but something was missing. Every time I scored a goal, I would look around to see if anyone had witnessed my moment of glory. I was searching for my parents so I could erase all memories of "goalie horror show." But my family was not there to watch my moments of fame.

The club championship was special because the final game was played under makeshift floodlights, and the whole neighborhood poured in to watch in the festive atmosphere. My team was in the final. It was a high-pressure match, and I had never played in front of that many people. Before the match, my team captain pointed to me and stated that he was relying on me to score and help my team.

The game started with a bang. Within minutes, a cross pass from the left came to me. I did not try to trap the ball, but instead shot it right into the goal. It was only three minutes into the match and I had scored the go-ahead goal. The crowd went crazy. My team surrounded me. Through all this, I tried to look at the sidelines to see if anyone from my family was there watching.

The rest of the half was uneventful, and we went to halftime with a one-goal lead. The second half was a story of missed opportunities. I had quite a few scoring opportunities, but I shot wide off the target every time. Five minutes from close, I was tackled hard inside the penalty box and the referee awarded a penalty kick. I placed the ball and looked at the goalie. It reminded me of eight-year-old Arjun standing under the bar. I walked back, turned, and walked toward the ball. I tapped it to the left of the goalie. It was a weak, feeble shot. The goalie dived to the left, anticipating the shot. The ball moved slowly, but right before the goalie could grab it, it hit something on the ground and changed directions. The goalie helplessly saw the feeble shot get in the goal. I screamed in delight. My team went crazy as victory was assured. In the middle of all this, I stopped celebrating. I left my teammates and walked over to the goalie. He was crushed and humiliated. I knew the feeling. I gave him my hand and pulled him to his feet. We patted each other on the back and the game resumed.

When I think back, I am not sure if I was screaming for scoring a goal or because it was such a relief to see my mistake happen to someone else.

Our team won the match and the championship. I got the highest-scorer trophy. That night at the dinner table, my brother and I were going over the match when Maiji commented, "You should have placed the penalty to the right of the goalie; that was his weak side."

My eyes lit up. Had she been there? Had she watched me score? I asked her, and she smiled but did not say anything. After dinner, as we were clearing the table, my Maiji walked past me and softly chanted, "Highest goal scorer! Highest goal scorer!" I felt goose bumps.

That night when I lay in bed, I could hear that chant over and over. Maiji had been there. She had seen me score. I had a big smile on my face.

~ Any moment for a child becomes a memory if there is someone to witness the moment. ~

DOCTOR, ENGINEER, OR LOSER
SECRET MEETING, KOLKATA, 1982

Growing up in India in the eighties gave me three career options: I could be an engineer, be a medical practitioner, or be considered a loser. Why were there only three choices? I do not know, but I know it was not for me to question why. Today, when I look back at my classmates from school, I see those who followed the path of engineering or medicine as well as those who made great lives of their own. But all of them have to admit the pressure they faced in the eighties if they were to choose a career path other than medicine or engineering.

Now let us get to how I chose my path. I could not stand the sight of blood, so practicing medicine for me was ruled out. I deduced that I could not be a loser either; hence I had no option other than to be an engineer. My father was a civil engineer who worked in a bank. Because my father was an engineer, it was another good step for a good, obedient, conforming oldest son to follow in his dad's footsteps. A blend of hard work and good luck got me admitted to the Indian Institute of Technology (IIT), Kharagpur.

I think back in utter amazement and disbelief about the night when the decision was made regarding which branch of engineering I would pursue. The reason I say the decision was made is because I had no role to play in that decision at all. My father and his friend sat down in the living room with glasses of whiskey. My father's friend was involved in the decision because his son had been admitted to the same university and was also awaiting a decision on what area of engineering he would pursue. The son and I were hanging out in a different room, contemplating our future lives away from home, while our parents were involved in a long discussion. For the two of us, it felt like we were waiting for a deliberating jury who would soon emerge with the verdict on our future lives. Strangely enough, neither of us worried about the impact of the decision on our lives. We trusted our parents to do the right thing. In the age of arranged marriages, I suppose one had to have faith in arranged education choices.

After their closed-door discussion, our parents called us into the room. We walked in and stood in anticipation as my friend's verdict was announced first. It was declared that he should pursue chemical engineering, as his dad was in the chemical business. It made perfect sense. Next, it was my turn. My father announced that I would pursue a career in aeronautical engineering.

Aeronautical engineering! I stood in the room in complete disbelief. What was it? Why me? Or better, why did they choose it for me? I hesitated as I mumbled out loud, enquiring about the decision. I do not remember whether the jury gave me a reason for the verdict or not, but I do remember there was a follow-up discussion about me and aeronautical engineering later on. My dad and his friend were very excited for me to become an aeronautical engineer. I listened attentively, but still it was not clear to me. I remember vaguely that the discussion had something to do with pilots or something.

The "conforming me" paused for a second, somewhat startled at the surprise verdict, but the pause lasted just a moment. I began preparing for my life away from home to become an aeronautical engineer.

~ At the beginning of a journey, the destination may not be that important. Starting the journey is all that matters. ~

AFTER LEAVING HOME

LIFE ENGINEERED
KHARAGPUR, INDIA, 1982

My engineering days in IIT Kharagpur may be different from that of any student who has ever graduated from that university. Day one at IIT, I saw a world of opportunities in front of me. Whether it was volunteer work, participating in a new sport, joining the student government, competing with the debate team, or acting in a play, I grabbed each and every opportunity with both hands. Of course, in the process, academics took the back stage, but I was doing well enough to make sure that I would graduate on time.

I started with hockey and soccer and soon made the university teams. Then one morning I woke up and wanted to join the debate team. I had never participated in a debate before, so practice started immediately. My practice went great, and very soon I realized I was good enough to pull it off—at least until I realized that a credible debater needed the right clothing. Even in those days I knew that without the right looks you are nothing.

That weekend I traveled back home and talked to Maiji. She looked at me through her glasses with a smile, then tucked her white sari around her waist and pulled a monster trunk out from under her bed. She went through her set of keys and slowly unlocked the trunk. Instantly, there was the smell of moth balls in the air. Inside the trunk, I could see layers and layers of clothing, all folded meticulously. She started her search and soon pulled out a blue sweater. It was the first sweater she had ever knitted for me. She could not resist taking out the sweater and holding it against me for a second before putting it back in the trunk. I guess she figured that the sweater had shrunk, for I am sure that in her eyes, I had never grown up.

Maiji found a pair of gray, pleated, baggy trousers. They had been custom tailored for my grandfather, who had worn them when he attended graduate school in London. As I held the woolen trousers in my hands, I wondered if my grandfather, too, had debated while wearing these trousers. Next, Maiji took out a white, long-sleeved shirt. She held it in her hands, hesitated for a second, and then handed it over to me. Maybe the clothes connected Maiji to some special memories. As I held my newly acquired clothes, Maiji pulled me close and gave me a long hug.

I was all set. Thanks to Maiji, I had my uniform, and a debater was born. More than the debate uniform, I found my connection with my late grandfather. The pants stayed with me for many years to come.

~ Heritage can come in any form as long as it connects you to who you are and where you came from. ~

SURROUNDED BY GIRLS
KHARAGPUR, INDIA, 1983

In my engineering college there were very few female students. In every batch of six hundred students there were three to five female students. This ensured that the female students got more than their fair share of attention from the rest of us, and it also caused its fair share of challenges in different areas. One of the areas it impacted the most was our college plays. The shortage of female students forced us to choose plays with very few female leads or actors.

In this environment came my next challenge for myself. I wanted to act in a play. And I wanted to act with two female leads, not just one. My reasoning was simple; it would be cool and noticeable. I approached my friend Bedo, who agreed to direct the play if I could find the cast. I searched and found two first-year girls to join our play, and, with Bedo's superb direction, our play was a big hit. The primary reason it was a hit was that everyone was curious to see two of the five new girls on campus, but still, not bad for my play debut.

My next play was far more serious. Bedo found a Bengali translation of Anthony Shaffer's *Sleuth,* a well-written drama, perfect for the two of us. He and I started rehearsal immediately on this two-actor (no actress) play.

The rehearsals were intense, and it was clear that, between the two of us, Bedo was the real actor. The day before the play, we started working on our stage setup. We needed some simple furniture and utensils, so I went to visit a friend who lived on campus. Her mom let us borrow some of her belongings, including a coffee table and glasses. The play went smoothly until we came to the part where I was supposed to go into a rampage and throw things around in a destructive manner. Being the natural actor I am, I started doing just that when I heard a voice from the audience. It was my friend's mom. I could clearly hear her utter, "Arjun, if you break any of my furniture or glasses, I will have to come down on that stage and smack you." I paused for a second and realized that even though I absolutely loved my friend's mom, I also knew she was quite capable of coming on stage and smacking me. As a result of this realization, the rampage was moderated and furniture was delicately overturned instead of thrown around. I was thrilled my friend's mom and the rest of audience did not have any more reason to scream at my performance.

When I think back to those days, I admire myself for going after *nirmal anand,* or pure happiness. Life had no worries. I would wake up every morning and think, "What have I not done yet that I want to try today?" In that pursuit of the untraveled path I would jump to a new path every day. Somehow, through all this, there was a strong force of moral values that steered me toward a path of goodness and away from danger or the dark side. At times, I feel my "sense of conforming" overshadowed my "force of moral values," but then again, I have nothing to regret. I lived life every day on my own terms, and the consequences were never negative.

~ It is fun to jump into the darkness of the future with no goals, no plans, and no expectations and just live in the moment. ~

DEAD DOG WINS THE ELECTION
KHARAGPUR, INDIA 1985

Near the end of my third year in my engineering college, I decided to run for the highest student office on campus. I ran for the position of student vice president, or VP. The position of president was held by a faculty member, and that made VP the highest office a student could hold on campus. Those days, the election usually featured a candidate who was slightly left of center and a candidate who was slightly right of center. There were already two candidates before I joined the race. Deba was the candidate who was slightly left of center, and Venky was the candidate slightly right of center. When I decided to join the race, I realized I was slightly more right of center than left. As that was surely going to result in a division of votes on the right, I realized there was very little chance for either me or Venky to win.

I vividly remember meeting with Venky at the Open Air Theater cafeteria. It was at eight in the evening and the cafeteria was empty. The meeting was supposed to be just between him and me, so we could discuss if one of us should step down from the election. I honored our agreement and showed up alone, but once I got to the meeting spot, I realized I had been ambushed. Venky was there with eight to ten of his supporters. All of them started bombarding me with reasons why I was the worst of the three candidates and I should drop out of the race immediately to give Venky a chance to win. It was a brutal meeting. They mocked me for being a rationalistic *Bong*. (*Bong* is the slang used to describe a resident of Bengal.) The debater in me tried to make my case, but I realized this meeting was set up to have only one outcome—for me to drop out of the race.

But I did not want to quit. I guess I always did better when quitting or losing seemed imminent, and on top of that, I was wearing my lucky pants worn by my late grandfather in many a tough day. I was trying to find light at the end of the tunnel to plan my escape route. Then a new strategy to get out of this jam came to me. I learned how to act stupid!

Since that day, acting stupid has helped me get out of numerous messy situations. To me, acting stupid is saying the same meaningless and unrelated thing over and over with statistical references my friends often called "rho zero," referring to zero correlation. Most of the time, it is a great way to defuse personal frustration and anger without making the situation worse. It also helps keep situations from escalating into a confrontation. For those on the other side, it is unexpected and baffling to react to. Finally, when people realize that that you are simply 100 percent stupid, they provide you with some mercy.

Now that I had indentified my strategy, I had to apply it. To anything Venky or his supporters said, I replied with the same answer with a smile, "But I will win." Finally after I had said my line umpteen times, there was silence in the cafeteria. Venky's supporters were not speaking anymore. They were staring at each other trying to decide what do to next. I seized the moment and got up. I walked around the room and shook hands with every one of his supporters, including the captain of my hockey team, and repeated one more time, "I am counting on your vote, as I will win."

The campaign process was very unique to me. Very soon, I realized that I had a group of friends who cared about me and my winning even more than I did. They worked day and night campaigning for me. I wore my white shirt and my grandfather's baggy gray pants and attended soapboxes and debates. Then there came the one incident that finally swung the election in my favor.

One of the girls on campus, who was one year junior to me, was bitten by a stray dog near the university's main gate. The security officers did their work by catching the dog immediately and tying it up to the gate. The security guards wanted to observe the dog to make sure it wasn't infected with rabies. After two days of being chained to the gate, the dog died. Everybody was worried about getting the girl who was bitten anti-rabies shots immediately. I personally was not sure if the dog had died because of rabies, or because it was tied to a gate without food and water for days, but that was not the right time to raise that issue. The challenge of the moment was to get the medication for the damsel in distress.

The medication for the anti-rabies shot was not available in Kharagpur and had to be procured from Kolkata, 120 kilometers from campus. The moment I heard about the girl's plight, I was on a train to Kolkata to get the medicine. Within eight hours, I was back with the medication. The girl and her friends gave me a hero's welcome and prepared an elaborate meal to thank me. As I enjoyed my elaborate meal, my image of "what a guy" was set in concrete. As the news spread, all the girls were ready to vote for me. In a campus where girls are few in number but very highly visible, their endorsement went a long way toward making me a feasible candidate.

Then came the actual election day. I had dozens of friends campaigning tirelessly to make sure every vote that had been promised was actually cast in my favor. Their efforts paid off. I won by thirteen votes in a triangular contest. The little right of the center had prevailed over the more right of center and left of center.

As I sat in the student gymkhana witnessing the election counting, it took me some time to realize that I had won, actually won, the election. I knew I won only because of the screams of my team of supportive friends, who were outside the gymkhana. I came out of the gymkhana with fists in the air to greet my friends. Soon I was surrounded by my jubilant friends and we started planning our victory procession.

In the middle of all this, my mind went back to that meeting with Venky's supporters at the empty Open Air Theater. As I thought of that evening, I smiled to myself and said, "I will win."

One of my supporters heard me and said, "Arjun, you have already won!"

I reached out for him and grabbed his arms and said, "I know, I know." Then I paused again as I said to myself, "I will win!"

Today I think back on how these events defined me. Being a true believer in Karma, I realize that we do not control what happens to us. What we control is how we react to those situations. A creative reaction and quick thinking, infused with a dose of humor, can be the difference between an adverse situation overcoming you and your overcoming an adverse situation. Professionally, this acquired skill has helped me in numerous situations, but the area this skill has benefited me most is in dealing with my daughter, Raka. And yet, even with all these preparations, life with Raka produced moments I just was not prepared for at all.

~ You do not control what happens in life. You simply control how you react to it. ~

JUST BROKEN STRINGS
KHARAGPUR, INDIA 1985

A few weeks after my election, I was expected to address the student body as the vice president elect. I had a friend who was the perfect person to write my address for me. Bhatto wrote a brilliantly eloquent speech, and I did my share to memorize and practice it in front of him. On the day of the speech, he and my friends were all excited for me to deliver the speech. Rightfully so, they felt this election was more of their win than my individual glory.

I got on stage. I was ready. Then I realized that something was odd. With the audience in the dark, I could hear them but could not see anyone. I was addressing a roar of invisible faces. I was not nervous; I was just in unfamiliar territory.

I started the speech exactly as it was written. In the second paragraph, however, I came to the part where I was supposed to bid farewell to the graduating class. The line written for me was, "Our seniors leave us, leaving behind broken hearts and torn strings." That was an incredibly well-written line. It would have worked for anyone else, but not me.

When I stared at the audience in the dark, I said, "torn hearts and broken strings." A few lines later, I realized that I was not making any sense and that I was not good at reciting a prepared speech. To Bhatto's dismay, I switched to my own speech and went on to say what was on my mind.

My speech was not as articulate as or anywhere close to the oratory excellence of Bhatto's speech, but I enjoyed and savored the moment. It was me—a little imperfect, a little stumbling, but straight from the heart.

I had found myself. Over time, I came to call this the gambler in me. It has become a signature of mine to get into a situation with a half-prepared solution, and then gauge the situation as I mold the final answer. This addiction to uncertainty would drive my career goals till September 2001, when a day with Raka made me realize the price of all this.

~ The same path is not for everyone. Uncertainty can be addicting, and any addiction has its price. ~

THAT AIRPLANE
KHARAGPUR, INDIA, 1986

Even though academics were not on my primary radar, it was an academic event that defined me for my future from that point on. In my final year of aeronautical engineering school, I was supposed find a solution for transporting a payload from point A to point B. The project involved working with different faculty members to find a solution. I worked with faculty members on aerodynamics, the aircraft structure, the propulsion, and other key areas. I have to confess that I made decent progress in each functional area but waited till the very end to put the final presentation of the project together.

Two days before the final presentation, I realized that my aircraft design was close to 1.2 miles long. I knew either I had broken the code for the next Nobel Prize or made the biggest goof in aeronautical engineering history. There was no doubt in my mind that I had not broken the code for a Nobel Prize. What followed were frantic meetings with different faculty members to discuss the parts of the project. In the process, I experienced the brilliance of each faculty member and how thorough they were in their individual areas of specialization.

I never figured out why my aircraft was 1.2 miles long, but I learned a lot about different functional areas of aeronautical engineering. What was a bigger education to me personally was learning that individual parts can never be bigger than the whole. I realized that a lot of us find comfort in focusing on parts since they are more tangible. Connecting to an imaginary big picture takes a leap of faith, and that throws a lot of us outside our comfort zones.

~ Focusing on the parts without a vision of the whole is like focusing on the journey without a vision of your destination. ~

THE DAYS AND MONTHS BEFORE 1993

SUMMONED TO AMERICA
PROVO, UTAH, 1988

I came to the United States to pursue my MBA at Brigham Young University in Provo, Utah, with only $320 in my pocket. It was a rude awakening to find that the cab fare from the Salt Lake City airport to Provo would cost me $75. I just could not sacrifice 25 percent of my net worth for a cab ride, so I waited till I found someone to give me a ride to the BYU campus. Over the years, I have often been asked why I came to Utah. The answer is very simple. I had applied to fifteen universities around the country. BYU was the only university that offered me a full scholarship and tuition waiver, an offer hard to refuse.

The first few days in the country of my dreams were simply enlightening. Friends who had come to the United States before me had bragged about the wall-to-wall carpets, the televisions, the cars, and the life of unlimited opportunities. What no one had told me was that, contrary to my expectations, I would *not* be able to afford a three-bedroom apartment, similar to what my company provided me, or have someone who would cook for me, clean my place, and who would do my laundry. I was really in a world of only me. On the one hand, the opportunities were mine and only mine, but on the other, I was responsible for all aspects of my life.

In Provo, I met Mac. He too was originally from India and was very kind to let me stay with him in his apartment, but there were some nuances. We could not go to the apartment till nightfall. My first entrance into the apartment with Mac was through the window. Then, when I went in for my first shower, I was greeted with bone-chilling, brutally cold water. I realized that Mac was a little behind on paying his landlord, and a few of the services had been withdrawn till he paid up.

Eventually I could afford my own room in an apartment that was an eight-block walk from campus. That's when I learned what brain freeze is. Growing up in India, I had never seen snow or ice nor experienced cold weather. I also was not picky with my looks, and after a shower I would towel-dry my hair and hand comb it, a process that worked great until one day in October in Provo, Utah. As always, I showered, towel-dried my hair, and followed up with a classy hand combing. I grabbed my books and assignments and dashed out for class.

As I was walking to class, I realized I was not feeling very well. My head was a little heavy, and I was getting a headache. I was worried that I might be coming down with something, but class was important, and I dashed on to school. Once I got to the Marriott School of Business, I realized I was not getting the regular warm greetings from my classmates as I walked down the corridor. Maybe they did not like me anymore.

It was one of my friends who stopped me and asked me to touch my hair. My first reaction was "ewww." There was all this very flaky hard stuff on my head. I rushed to the restroom and was startled to see that my wet hair had a layer of icy freeze on it. It took me a while to realize what had happened. Though I was quite amused, I was in utter disbelief.

I was not at home anymore. I was more than halfway across the globe in a land where everything was foreign to me. The question that came to my mind repeatedly after that was, "Do I belong here?" I never answered the question. I just staggered forward.

The stagger transformed into brisk walking, and soon I was running professionally as I realized that even in this unfamiliar land, I could deal with life using the skills I had acquired as a child. When I was growing up, Maiji always told me that when I found myself in deep water, I should realize that I have the capability to swim out of that situation. She was very spiritual and told me God was never cruel or unkind. He would only put me in the middle of an ocean if He was sure I could swim out to safety. All I needed to do was believe in myself and my capabilities and then put all my effort into moving my hands and feet to swim away. Effort is everything. Results just happen.

~ Sometimes one needs a little brain freeze to be woken up. ~

RESCUE ME
PROVO, UTAH, 1988

When I came to the United States, I went through some of the toughest days in my life. I hardly had any money, and there was a huge glitch with my financial aid from the university. As the situation unfolded, I started getting scared, as I had only $320 to last me for three to four months till my financial aid situation got resolved.

I called Maiji on a long-distance international call. She listened to my problem and then asked me how much I was paying to call her. When I told her that it was close to $1.25 a minute, she asked me to hang up the phone immediately. I was hurt and quite disappointed as Maiji withdrew her helping hand. I couldn't believe that my Maiji did not try to rescue me.

Two weeks later, I got a letter from Maiji. In that letter she gave me the mantra, "*Harayo na himmat, bishoriyo no Ram*" or, "Do not lose your determined spirit, and do not forget God." She believed in me.

In her next letter, she told me again that she believed God would never throw me into the middle of an ocean unless He was sure I knew how to swim. Yes, I had to move my hands and feet to get to the shore, but once I got there I would be a stronger man. She was telling me that she believed in my capabilities and strength. She also was inspiring me to act and take charge of the situation so I could come out with flying colors.

I could not believe the change in Maiji. This was the same person who, until four years back, used to wake me up in the mornings. Now she was leaving me alone? Now she trusted me to act on my terms? On one hand, I was happy to be treated like an adult. On the other hand, I missed Maiji's presence next to me.

~ Believe in those you love and inspire them to achieve the impossible. ~

JUST MARKET IT
PROVO, UTAH, 1988

In the Marriott School of Management at BYU, I was obsessed with becoming the best. I was driven. Unlike during my engineering days, academics were a priority and the only priority. I was there with a purpose. If you did not find me with my study group, you would find me touring the offices of the faculty to make sure I was on the good list in their books. I was truly a brownnoser and workaholic. After my first case write-up in marketing, the professor summoned me to his office after class. I knew it could not be good to be summoned to meet with a professor, but I was wrong. While I was in his office, he told me he was amazed by my paper. He felt I was one of the best he had ever taught, and he seriously suggested I major in marketing. I was not used to academic praises, so this professor's words stuck in my mind. Soon I decided to follow his path and chose marketing. In one of my lonely nights in Provo, I started thinking: after I graduated I would become an aeronautical engineer in the field of marketing. Yes, I was my dad's son. Just like he had to explain all his life what he was doing as a civil engineer in a successful banking career, I too had created my own conversation starter.

After one semester in Utah, I went to India and got married. Gopa and I had known each other for four years and shared a common dream of pursuing higher education in the United States. For those of you wondering, it was not an arranged marriage. But even though it was a self-arranged marriage, once we decided to get married, our families took over the details of the process.

The day our marriage was registered, Maiji, my parents, and Gopa's family were all sitting together with the marriage registrar. It was a solemn occasion blessed by the elders. The marriage registrar was a funny man, and just before Gopa and I signed on the dotted lines, he asked me if I was sure. I paused and looked at Maiji. Then I giggled and said to Maiji, "Maiji, this is the last chance. All through life I adored you. You look more beautiful than ever, and all you need to say is yes and I will marry you."

Everyone was shocked at my statement, especially Gopa's family, who did not know my crazy side. Maiji was speechless for a moment and then blushed at this unwanted attention. It lasted just a moment before I got a smack on my head. I had my answer. As I signed the marriage certificate, I realized again what Maiji was to me, and I guess this statement was my way of paying tribute to her. I hope she realized that.

Gopa traveled to the United States with me and soon started her masters program in microbiology. With both spouses going through school, and my being obsessed with being the best, life for our family was defined more by school and less by a home.

There were a lot of new things in my life. Utah, marketing, and marriage all were new to me. I was trying my best to juggle all these new things and set my life and career up for success. Then came the ultimate of newness—we bought a car. It was a ten-year-old Subaru station wagon, stick shift. Before I bought the car I went to the driver's license office for my learner's permit. All I had was a two-wheeler driver's license from India. When I went to the driver's license office in Provo, I was given a written test, which I passed. Next, an official approached me and stated that he was ready to take me out for the driving test. I was not sure what was going on. I had never driven a car. I had never sat behind the steering wheel of a car. How could I take a driving test?

The officer told me that I should have no problems, as I had been driving for four years in India. That was when I realized that my driver's license from India was for both cars and two-wheelers. When I filled out the application in Jamshedpur, India, all I had wanted was a license to drive my two-wheel scooter. The license agent told me that the application would cost only 120 rupees. That was not bad. Then he said for fifty rupees more I could also get an auto license. That was not a bad idea. I agreed. I had no idea that my paying an extra fifty rupees and getting an auto driver's license would come to haunt me in Provo, Utah. As I hesitated, the officer came to my rescue. He realized my hesitation and stated, "You should maybe come back another day when you are ready."

I was relieved. Then he added, "Maybe that day will be more auspicious for you." From that word I guessed that he might have dealt with people from India before. When I finally had my learner's permit in hand, we bought the car. Needless to say, the day we picked up the car and drove it home from Orem, Utah, was a big challenge.

Of course when I talk about my days in Utah, everyone gets curious about how I got to the land of Mormons. I have to confess that I did not know about Mormonism when I first arrived in Utah. Even though I had signed a contract to obey the principles of a Mormon life, I did break one rule often and had coffee in my apartment. Yes, it was a little tough being one of the few "brown people" in the state of Utah, but when everyone asks about the pressure I may have felt to convert to Mormonism, I cannot think of one instant when I felt pressured during my stay. Instead, what touched me was the family life in Utah and how all my friends and their families adopted me with no questions asked. At first, I used to use the F-word very casually as part of the British influence in my speech. Howard, a friend, realized that I had little hope to change and hence taught me a whole new set of words that start with F, but which end differently. The best word was of course "farther" or "faaarther"; "fuun" was another word I used often.

There were others who reached out and helped me settle into my new life. When I think back to those days and how each of them reached out to help me into this new land, I believe I simply could not have pulled it off without them. I was doing well in reacting to life situations in Utah, but as I think back, I ask myself what the most important thing was that I could focus on. Was preparing for my career and professional life the most important thing in my life? Did

I take my marriage for granted? Was my addiction to seeking and reacting to uncertainty driving my life a bit too much?

~ Give life a chance, because only then will magic happen. That being said, know what is important in life. ~

FOOD IN MY LIFE
WICHITA, KANSAS, 1990

Once I was ready to graduate from Brigham Young University's MBA program, I was prepared for my first job. Pizza Hut corporate had come to campus to interview candidates. I went to their presentation to get a slice of free pizza and a free pink T-shirt. I never imagined how big they were or what their corporate office looked like, but following the slideshow I was instantly interested in working for them. After my classmate Brad took a job with them, I flew in for an interview. I quickly became an aeronautical engineer with an MBA working in the restaurant industry.

I took the job, and I worked hard. I was trying hard to impress everyone, and I was always in a rush. When I look back, I do not understand why I was in that rush. It seemed like I was like Alexander the Great, wanting to conquer the world in just a few days with no time to settle in and enjoy my accomplishments.

My professional career progressed after I realized that I could not allow people to slow my advancement because of my accent. Initially I was taken aback when the only negative item on my performance appraisal was, "needs to get rid of his accent." At the same time, another employee in the company came from Australia. He too spoke in an accent that was foreign and quite different. People would call his accent "cute." I realized that I just needed to slow down.

Growing up in Bengal, India, I spoke British English with a *Desi-*

Bengali accent. When I came to the United States, I learned that I spoke too fast, so I slowed down. I still struggled with the American way of pronunciation, though. The first company I worked for was called Executive Excellence. While there I could not pronounce *Executive* in the true spirit of the word. When I answered the phone, "Executive Excellence, this is Arjun," people would conclude that they had reached the premier execution service in the nation. I also could not pronounce the V in Vickie. Instead I said, "We-ckie," and of course that did not flatter my department assistant, Vickie. Another tough one was the letter P. The way I pronounced it, it would come across as B. No wonder over the years my ex-wife, Gopa, has gotten numerous credit cards under the name Goba. The worst of all was aluminum. That is one I only recently solved when I realized that in the United States, it is spelled aluminum with no *i* after the *n* as it is in Britain. I guess the folks who came across the ocean believed in simplifying the words. Colour became color, and aluminium became aluminum.

After futile attempts to correct my pronunciations, I decided to accept myself for who I am and live with it. I was determined to talk more slowly and pay a lot of attention to people as I talked to them. If my audience did not understand me, I would use synonyms to get my thoughts across. My job was to communicate, and that I did.

I was starting to figure out how corporate America works. In my early days in corporate America, I did a little research to find out what variables were associated with success. After a lot of statistical analysis, I realized that the key attributes defining a higher propensity to succeed included being a white male, being five feet and eight inches or taller, and walking fast. I did not initially understand the implications of my incredible insight until I was sitting in my cubicle one day and realized that an average cubicle wall is five feet and seven inches high. That means if you are a white male who is visible over the walls of the cubicles and you walk fast, which translates into a hustle, you are perceived to be a mover and shaker, and hence successful. After that, I sat in my cubicle and wondered. I was male. That was good. I would never be white. I would never get to 5'8" or beyond in height. So by my calculations, my only chance for success was to carry my folders in my hand above my head and walk fast.

Maybe then I would get noticed. I have to confess, I did actually try it a few times.

I do not know whether it was carrying my folders high or other things I was doing, but once I got less desperate, I started moving up the corporate ladder. I moved into bigger and bigger cubicles, then finally into offices. Offices with windows were a final reward. I was advancing rapidly in my career. I moved quickly from Pizza Hut to Boston Market, to Einstein Bros Bagels, to Papa John's. My résumé needed to be updated every six months. I had more responsibilities, I was making more money, and I was in positions of power. But what was all that for? What was I really trying to accomplish?

One day I was watching Charlie Chaplin's *Modern Times.* The movie starts with a classic scene with thousands of factory workers leaving work. The next scene blends into thousand of cattle walking together without any individual direction. I started thinking about whether or not I was part of a herd, all of whom were walking briskly in the same direction, thinking the journey would take me to where I wanted to go. Had I become a cow following my herd? Had I taken my level of conforming to new heights? My life was epitomized by the phrase "living in the present," but I paid little attention to where I wanted my future to go. Career changes to move forward were automatic. Stopping to smell the roses never crossed my mind.

~ Be watchful of adverse forces that try to change your core. ~

MESSY CHILDREN
WICHITA, KANSAS, 1991

Gopa and I had settled into our first apartment in Wichita, Kansas, and done the best we could to decorate the place. We got our furniture from Bassett; it was the first time we did not have used furniture. Soon the new mattresses and the dining table arrived. It was nothing fancy, but we were proud of it. It was a huge step forward from the student housing of Wymount Terrace in Provo.

One evening, we invited a friend and his family over for dinner. They had an adorable little baby, so as a part of my social interaction, I tried to hold the baby. From the way I was holding him, you could very easily see how uncomfortable I was. It was the soccer player in me trying to hold the odd shaped ball called a football in America. I also realized, in my brief moment of holding the baby, that it is a myth that babies smell good. This baby smelled of stale poop, and stale poop smell is not at all good.

Everything went well till after dinner. The baby's diaper exploded. No wonder I smelled poop when I held the baby. As the mom tried to fix it, the smelly poop went everywhere into the carpet. I could not believe that the worried mom first tried to attend to the baby instead of worrying about our carpet. After she cleaned the baby and put a new diaper on, the tired mom tried to clean the carpet the best she could. As I was sitting across from her I could distinctly count the numerous areas in the carpet that the mom had missed. It was clearly disgusting.

After they left that night, I was out with heavy duty carpet cleaners. I still could not believe the amount of mess this baby caused and that I was cleaning up after it. I was appalled that parents could just allow their babies to mess up like that. Eventually I realized that once you have your own baby in your arms, none of the poop smells matter anymore. But for me, that feeling would not arrive for two more years.

~ Mistakes of today are just a stepping stone to future learning. ~

1993

WAKE UP! WAKE UP! WICHITA, KANSAS, 1993

For the first time in my life, I did not know what hit me. Raka was due to arrive on September 26, 1993, and Gopa and I were getting ready. We were building our first home in Wichita, which we would be able to move into by September 22. After that, we would get settled for a week before we welcomed our new baby. All this sounded like a perfect plan, and it was going great till fate decided to take over.

September 14, 1993, 7:30 AM
I awoke from sleep and felt I had one of those mysterious illnesses. I had no fever, I had no cold, I had no body aches, yet I just could not get out of bed. The prescription for that ailment was written on the ceiling as I lay in bed. Call in sick.

I left a voice mail for my department assistant and stayed in bed. The Kansas sun was rising outside our bedroom window, trying to sneak through the off-white vertical blinds, but I was determined to stay in bed and not allow the sun to wake me. Finally, at 10:00 AM, I clearly heard the calm yet determined voice of my wife. She uttered those words that can change a man's life.

"My water just broke."

I jumped out of bed. I felt like the fire-truck driver who had been trained for that moment. The first call had just come in. This was my moment of fame. All I needed to do was take my wife to the hospital. But before we left home, I had to get something. What was it?

As I brushed my teeth, I kept thinking over what I needed to take with me. The hospital kit was ready by the door downstairs, but I was supposed to add tennis balls to the bag. As I brushed I ran to the basement to get some tennis balls, but there was a dilemma. Did I take used tennis balls, or did I open a new can of tennis balls that cost $3.99? After a moment I emerged from the basement with a new can of three fresh tennis balls.

I changed and got ready. As I waited for my wife to get ready, I planned the route to St. Francis Hospital. Out on Frontage Road, left on Kellogg Street, and then ... and then I could figure out the rest. Suddenly I saw the cover of the video we had watched the night before, *Untamed Heart*. The video was still in the VCR, so as I got it out and put it in the box I began re-routing in my mind. How long would it take to drop off the video at Blockbuster and then get to the hospital?

All this diversion planning stopped when my wife walked down the stairs. The Plymouth Voyager was ready. I helped her to the car and gently backed the car out of the garage. The sun shone in the sky above as I drove onto Kellogg Street. I looked in the rearview mirror and realized that the next time I drove the backseat would not be empty. I smiled. A feeling rose from deep in my heart like I had never felt before; it was that pure happiness from deep within. I kept driving.

September 14, 1993, close to noon
We checked into the exact room we had been shown during our visit to St. Francis Hospital. Gopa was progressing slowly with her two best friends next to her. They were like two mother hens protecting their offspring. One had the uncanny ability of just staring at Gopa's face and knowing what she felt or needed. She would massage my wife's forehead and hold her hand. She would smile softly and utter words of encouragement in the most endearing form. The other, a super doctor in her field, was making sure all the medical attention was there as needed.

As I sat across the room in a comfortable seat with my legs propped up on the leg rest, I had my first indication of the imminent miracle. However, I was too caught up in the worries of work, and in thinking of how to get the news to family back in India, to be able to enjoy the moment.

Today when I think back, I realize that there really was a miracle in the air. My life would change forever. To mark the miracle, two angels had appeared as witnesses. I am very bad with names and memories, but today as I look back, I can still see the hospital room, with my wife on the bed, and the two angels next to her, protecting her, as she got ready for childbirth.

September 15, 1993, 3:08 AM

It was a long night. After 10:00 PM, I knew the moment would arrive at any time. Finally at 1:00 AM, the doctor came in and, after a brisk inspection, said that we must get ready for a C-section. I was scared. I was scared for my wife. I was scared for my daughter who was ready to come to us. I was scared for myself, to have to witness the surgery.

I went in and sat in the designated seat next to my wife as the doctors prepared for the C-section. I do not remember the details of the surgery or how long it took, but I made it.

Then life appeared. I saw Raka for the first time when she had just come out of her mother as the doctors were rushing her to a corner table to make sure everything was all right. There was urgency in the air. I asked the attending doctor if it was a boy or a girl. In haste he stated, "I do not know."

I could not believe what I had just heard. Our pediatrician does not know if our baby is a boy or a girl! Wow! I could not imagine anyone who worked for me surviving the day with that kind of inefficiency. I looked at my watch. The time stopped at 3:08 AM.

After a few moments, it was announced that we had a baby girl. Raka was here. She had arrived. I remember her very first accomplishment: she peed. Yes, she peed. I was elated. I jumped around and thought, "My daughter peed! My daughter peed!" I was proud of my little daughter. Yes, she peed. That night was marked with more first accomplishments of this amazing child. As the nurses took her to the nurse's station, I looked at her through the glass window. Isn't she adorable? She was looking at me through her closed eyes. She was at peace. Her tiny fingers moved a little. I was in love.

Along with love came fear. I had heard so many stories of babies getting exchanged in the hospital. I would stare through the glass window to make sure our baby was fine. In that Kansas hospital, I made sure that the only brown baby was ours.

The name Raka came primarily from Gopa's insistence that we find a two-syllable name of Indian origin that would not get butchered in school or beyond. I liked that logic. After a lot of research, we came to Raka. In India, every full moon has a distinctive name. The *purnima* (full moon) on which Krishna was born is called the Raka *purnima*. That is the day the sky is the brightest. As we held Raka, we realized that even though Raka was not born on the Krishna full moon, it was our brightest day.

I spent the next few days in the hospital holding her and feeling her shrink into my chest. I remember all my work clothes had stains near my shoulder because my baby also drooled. Even today I look at my pictures, and I can see drool stains on my coat. Somehow, Raka liked drooling on my left shoulder more than my right shoulder. Was it because my heart was on the left?

The Voyager got us back home uneventfully. On the way, we stopped at the neighborhood K-Mart for some diapers. That was Raka's first car stop. The next stop was home.

The days that followed were marked with more firsts. I remember her first bath. Everything was all set: the tiny blue bathtub was there on the bathroom counter, the tiny towels and lotion bottle stood around, waiting to witness this occasion, and I was holding Raka in my right arm in what I was told was the football grip (one of the few things I had retained as I dozed off in Lamaze class). What happened next, I was not at all prepared for.

The first drop of water touching her cute baby butt made her scream, but then she stretched and nearly jumped out of my football grip. To regain stability, I grabbed her with both hands; I called it the hockey grip. After that, all baths featured a hockey grip.

Since then I have watched the movie *Untamed Heart* quite a few times. I do not feel it was a coincidence that we watched that movie the night before Raka was born. When I try to remember whether I returned the movie to Blockbuster Video, I am not sure. Either way, Blockbuster Video never charged us.

~ Fools plan because they do not know what is coming their way. ~

SNOOZING!
GOLDEN, COLORADO, 1995

A few weeks after Raka was born I went back to work, and my schedule quickly returned to normal. I was traveling all over the country on business, but each city was the same. Every hotel seemed to have the same bed and the same wake-up call person: Los Angeles, Rochester, Chicago, Austin, Orlando, and so on.

Yes, I missed Raka. On every trip I would stop somewhere and get Raka a new dress or a T-shirt or a battery-powered dog that flipped backward. By her second birthday, she had T-shirts from a dozen states.

My relationship with my wife started to stray, and as the years passed, Raka was growing up, growing into a young lady. I was in Denver, and Raka was in Wichita with her mother. I saw her only a few times a month, but my moments with her were precious. I remember the first time she learned to signal a touchdown. She was sitting on her plastic bike. I said, "Touchdown!" and she raised both hands in the air. She wanted to impress her dad, and she did. More touchdowns followed.

I rushed through life, satisfied with recalling an occasional touchdown signal by Raka. I would fill the void when I was away by looking at pictures of her and by repeatedly replaying the touchdown signal. Today when I sit back and reflect on those days of my life, I realize I am not smart enough to figure it out. However, I do have questions based on my own experiences:

- Why is it that men go after power and glory more than spending time at home to watch their babies grow?
- Why is it that men only measure their lives by money, promotions, the size of their offices, and the kinds of cars they drive?
- Why it is that men never stop to think what matters in the long run?
- Why is it that men invest all their time in a company that is sure to let them go one day?
- Why do men not invest time in their daughters, instead, who will never fire them?

~ Parenting is not just watching a few touchdowns on a highlight reel. ~

MY BROTHER'S WEDDING
MUMBAI, INDIA, 1996

I grew up in Kolkata with my brother, Oni, who is four years my junior. As we grew up, I defined new rules for conforming, and he rewrote the rules of no rules. From early childhood he was proud and confident in being himself. His hair was unruly, he had a pierced ear, and his clothing was sloppy. I was amazed at the strength of his friendships. He was hanging out with friends when I was in study groups with my geeky buddies. I was nervous as I asked permission from my parents to go out. He used to just inform my parents he was going out.

Through all this, I simply adored my brother.

My brother and I were at our creative best when we were together. I remember the time we were grounded on Diwali night. Diwali is the festival of lights, and we had done something evil that got us sentenced to the rooftop with no fireworks. That was not nearly enough to stop us from celebrating. We started assembling empty shoe boxes and other paper. We stacked them all neatly in a pile on the roof and set fire to it. Once the bonfire was going wild, we painted our faces with ashes and danced around the fire in a frenzy. Of course, the consequences were not in our favor when our parents found out about the fire.

Another time we were grounded we were sent to the backyard. It was boring for both of us to sit there in the backyard and do nothing, so we invented a new game. We stood ten feet apart and threw pebbles at each other. A direct hit was plus one point. If you moved to avoid a hit, that was minus two points. Neither of us was stupid enough to get minus points. Over time, the pebbles were turning into rocks and our aims were getting better and we were scoring a lot of points. Fortunately, Maiji intervened and brought an untimely end to the game just before we headed into a sudden death tiebreaker.

Growing up, my brother had tons of friends, and quite a few of them were girls. I did not know his seriousness with any particular girl till Rachna came into his life. All I knew was that he was serious about Rachna, a smart young lady who graduated from my brother's university.

Then I got a phone call from my parents, informing me that my brother was getting married. My parents told me the marriage would take place in Mumbai, and then there would be a reception in Kolkata. It was a phone call during which I listened to what they had to say and then uttered a deep "Ohhh." The next morning, I was off to Minneapolis on a business trip.

When I look back, I cannot recall the year my brother got married. I do not think I even called my brother on the day he got married. The exact date of the wedding or the reception did not register in my mind. On the wedding day, I was not homesick. I was not mentally visualizing every step of the wedding ritual of my brother and his bride. I had no regrets. I was working on a project that would put me closer to my next corporate promotion. I guess I had passed the test of corporate commitment and focused on the work at hand. Of course, when I think back, this is one of my biggest regrets. I really wish I could change that day, but more than anything, I want to go back and sit and interview me on one of those days. I want to understand what my value system was and why I had no regrets. I really want to understand what had hardened me so much. I know it did not happen overnight, but how did I miss the symptoms of gradual decay?

Even today, I have my brother's wedding card next to my desk. The square card printed on an off-white paper with ornate design somehow survived numerous moves and still sits next to my desk. Maybe it is still waiting for me to respond to the RSVP request.

~ Life does not allow reversing; instead, it allows regretting. ~

1994 TO 2001

ALL BLUE
MUMBAI, INDIA, 1996

When Raka was nearly three years old, she and I took our first trip to India to visit family. The moment we landed in India, my brother Oni and his wife Rachna fell in love with Raka. When we were finally settled at Oni and Rachna's home, I pointed to a blue sticker on the wall and asked Raka what color it was. Little Raka came, hid her head shyly in my feet, and said, "Blue," without looking at anyone else. Oni and Rachna were completely impressed. Just to impress them again I pointed to a small patch of a poster on the wall and asked Raka again. Raka stated with confidence again, "Blue."

Whatever doubt Oni and Rachna had in their minds about Raka's brilliance was put to rest. That night after Raka had gone to bed, Oni and I were catching up. Oni could not wait to ask me how we had taught all these things to Raka. I hesitated for a moment, and then decided to let my brother in on the secret. I explained to Oni that the trick was in selecting what color you wanted Raka to identify, as Raka would always answer "blue" to the question, "What color is it?"

Next day Oni took Raka to work. The little princess was completely at ease with her favorite Oni Kaka. (*Kaka* means uncle in Bengali.) From time to time, Oni Kaka would ask Raka, "Raka, what is the color of that book?"

Raka would smile and say, "It is blue." Everyone around Oni

would be impressed and Raka would dash to Oni Kaka for a big hug.

~ Asking the right question is all that matters. ~

SPELLING BEES
DENVER, COLORADO, 1996

Raka was three. Once we had established that Raka was brilliant in identifying colors, next it was her turn to spell. This was another area Raka excelled in from early childhood. I would get a list of words to help Raka practice her spelling, and Raka was patient and cooperative as her mother and I worked with her on the word list. We started with monosyllabic words and slowly progressed to multisyllabic words. Every Friday, when Raka got her week's assignments back, we went through her scores together. If she missed a word or two, we would pounce on them and help Raka relearn those words.

One day I was driving Raka to school. She was safely in her seat in the back. I was already in work mode and planning my day in my mind. I would drop off Raka at school, and then take the inner streets to bypass traffic so that I could get to work in time. NPR was playing in the background. Raka tried a few times to make me play her favorite music cassette. I told her repeatedly, "In a minute, baby." After a few failed attempts, Raka seemed to give up and contented herself with looking outside, counting cars, and singing.

Then all of a sudden she said, "Dad, I can spell …" The second part of the sentence was lost in the background noise in the car. I nodded my head and looked back at her through the rearview mirror. Her bright eyes were all lit up. She was excited.

I smiled back at her and said, "I love you, baby."

"I love you too, Dad," was her response. Then we continued with our bidding war on our love. Our bidding war was an exercise in mathematical learning. I would say, "I love you three," and Raka would say, "I love you four." It would go on till I said, "I love you infinity." That usually marked the end of the game as I had convinced Raka that no one could beat infinity. Over time Raka learned the word "googolplex." It was her way of ending the game on a winning note.

That day, the game was going on as scheduled. The traffic was bad, and we had progressed to the sixties. Both of us wanted the game to continue, as we had not used the words *infinity* or *googolplex* yet. In the middle of our game, Raka looked at me and said again, "Dad, I can spell *hibernate*." I was impressed and asked her to spell the word. The little girl closed her eyes and was in full concentration as she began confidently, "H-I-B-E-R." She paused and opened her eyes to make sure I was listening, and then finished with, "N-A-T-E."

I was impressed. "Wow, baby, that is impressive."

We were pulling into her school, and I did not get a chance to ask her where she had learned this word. That day when I went to work, the first thing I told my coworker, Vance, was that Raka knew how to spell hibernate. Vance was impressed too.

Since that day, Raka asked me the same question many a time: she would prompt me to ask her to spell *hibernate,* and I would gladly do it. Today, when I think back, I realize most of the time when she would prompt me to ask her to spell the word, I was distracted with work. Was it a coincidence that anytime I was not paying attention to her she prompted me to ask her to spell that particular word? Was she trying to tell me something? Even if she was trying to tell me something by uttering "H-I-B-E-R-N-A-T-E," I have to confess that I never caught on.

~ Signs and signals are around us. We have to be ready to acknowledge them. ~

A STAR IS BORN
DENVER, COLORADO, 1997

Raka was three and a half years old. The half was very important to her. When I asked her how old she was, she would pop open three fingers, then very carefully use both hands to open a fourth finger halfway. She was always full of smiles. Those days when I asked her what her name was, she would say Raka Sona Princess Misti-hashi Sen. *Sona* is a term of endearment and *misti-hashi* translates to sweet smile. It was the perfect name for her. Even today, when she smiles, the world lights up around her. I remember that smile she had put on my face as her mom and I drove to the hospital, and I saw the empty backseat for the last time.

One evening, Gopa and I took her to an Indian cultural function. It was the first time we had attended a function like that in Denver. Here I need to give you some background information on Indians in the United States. In India we have twenty-six states, and most states have their own language. To help you understand the magnitude of their differences, each language has its own alphabets and numbers. Hence, when I was in India and traveled to a different state, I could not read the bus numbers unless they were written in English. A wise man once characterized India as Unity in Diversity.

As Indians travel to the United States, they often hold on to their diversity more than their unity. Indians from different states only gather together with Indians who originate from the same state. There is very little contact beyond the state-origin lines among immigrant *Desis,* or Indians settled in the United States. I come from the state of West Bengal, one of the eastern states in India. The capital of the state is Calcutta, recently renamed Kolkata. The state language is Bengali, and in Denver, there is a social group of Bengalis (people from Bengal, India) called Milone. It was with this group that we gathered for our social event.

Once you enter the world of Milone, you leave the adopted culture of the United States behind and rush back to practices from home. Men gather around only with other men, trying to solve the world's problems. Each starts discussing his plans to send his kids to college. Women gather with women, showcasing their new saris and jewelry. Here is a secret I learned: A woman cannot wear the same sari more than once to a gathering, and if she does, others really do notice. Indian men, on the contrary, are not that sharp. I have worn the same pants and shirt to numerous parties and no one has noticed.

In the midst of the male gathering and the female fashion parade, the kids get to run around and be kids. The cultural program always starts forty minutes late and begins with the children's performances. It is very sweet to see young children on stage, dancing, singing, or reciting poems. What is an equally intriguing show is to see the mothers stand in front of the stage and mouth the words to the kids. You can see the stress and tension in the faces of the mothers as their children perform. The fathers, on the other hand, are the calmer lot. They jostle for a position to place their camcorders so they can record their kids' performances.

After the children's performances comes the torturous part when adults take the stage. I always enjoy watching kids perform, showcasing their enthusiasm and budding talent, but when adults forget that talent skipped them but perform anyway, the only way I survive is by chanting, "Encore!" in mockery from the back.

Now back to one particular performance on that specific evening. Raka was dressed in a beautiful Indian outfit. We walked in with her, and as Raka's mom chatted with other women, I held Raka's hand and met the other men. Raka was anxiously looking at other young faces, ready to dash out.

At that moment, the cultural performances started. A young girl was on stage who was supposed to dance to the tune of an Indian song. The girl was beautifully dressed with fresh flower garlands her mother had surely made for her. She was standing in the middle of the stage when the music started. She made a few hand movements, and then she froze. Her father was on the left of the stage and her mother was on the right of the stage, each trying to encourage her to perform. It was hilarious to see their encouragement turn from words, to prompting gestures, to quite curt scolding. The gathered crowd was more understanding. They had seen this happen before. They would silently wait for the song to end and then clap politely.

All of a sudden, there was energy in the air. Everyone in the room began clapping with the song. Some even whistled in excitement. When I looked up, I saw that our daughter was on stage. I had no idea when she had managed to walk away from me, but our daughter was dancing wildly on stage, and the other girl, too, was now dancing with Raka. As a dad, when I watched my little princess dance, I was proud. She was moving body parts in her dance that I did not even know she had. The dance ended with wild applause, and Raka came to me and said, "Dad, I was good, wasn't I?"

Yes, she was good. She was always good. She is always good.

~ A star is always born. It just takes time for fans to discover the star. ~

71

AM I GAY?
DENVER TO CINCINNATI FLIGHT, 1997

Raka was four, and she had moved with her mother to Denver, Colorado. On a business trip to Rochester, I decided to take Raka with me. Raka and I were in the middle seats of the crowded Conair plane en route to Cincinnati. It all started after she finished her meal and started playing with her two Barbies. To me, the actions of the two Barbies seemed inappropriate. Let me rephrase that: they were very inappropriate.

I was disappointed with my thoughts. I was the father of a four-year-old daughter. How could my mind work that way? I was seriously ashamed of myself. My mind was sorting through these thoughts when Raka broke the silence with, "Dad, my Barbies are gay."

I did not hear that. Even if I heard it, I wanted to ignore what Raka had said, hoping she would move on to something else. No, this was not happening. I was not equipped to deal with this. She was just four.

The illusions dissipated when Raka asked me, "Dad, are you listening?" and then repeated, "I am sure my Barbies are gay."

Now I was on the spot and in the spotlight. I was sure everyone around me had stopped doing what they were doing and were all focused on me and only me. All that was left was for the Captain to pick up the microphone and announce, "Ladies and gentlemen, may I have your attention please! The gentleman sitting in seat 10B will soon announce his verdict on his daughter's Barbies. The question before the gentleman is this: Are her Barbies gay?"

I was alert. Before the next set of more elaborate questions could come out of Raka, I looked at her and smiled softly. I gave her a warm hug and asked her in a tone that was close to whispering, "Why do you think this way?"

It seems Raka was waiting for this question. She told me immediately that there was a new girl in her school. Her mother and her mother's partner came to drop her at school, and the family was very affectionate. As they dropped the child at school, the whole family exchanged affectionate embraces, and after enquiring, Raka learned that the kid's mom and her partner were gay.

After I listened to her story, I breathed a sigh of relief. It was not that bad. Yes, I am sure I can think of a thousand reasons it could be worse. I looked at her and whispered again, "It is OK. There is nothing to worry about."

Raka looked at me, surprised. She said, "I know, Dad, that there is nothing wrong with being gay. I know it is okay." I was somewhat relieved with her statement. I just did not want this conversation to go any further. That was when she continued her questioning, "Dad, am I gay?"

I was startled. What was she talking about? She should not even talk about hugging, let alone kissing, and never about sex. Instead, she was asking if she was gay. I told her, "No, baby." There was a strong emphasis on *baby*. I was seriously hoping that the strong showing of affection would distract her from this subject, but this was not my lucky day.

Raka thought for a while, and then asked me, "How are you so sure, Dad?" There was no emphasis on *Dad*. She was asking the question because she was genuinely quite puzzled. I realized that in my effort to explain things to her, I was digging a deeper hole for myself, so I decided to use the adult card. It is the ultimate "get out of jail free" card.

I told Raka, "Please do not worry. I am an adult, and I know these things. When you grow older you will know, too. Now it is time for you to take a brief nap before we land in Cincinnati."

I was very proud of myself. I pulled her tiny body to me and had her head rest on my hands. I started patting her sides in rhythmic motion to make her fall asleep. At last, the crisis was averted. Arjun, super dad, saves the day. I kept thinking it was not that bad. Then lightning hit me. Raka slowly raised her head to my shoulder and bent her neck as she looked at me. I sensed disaster even before she opened her mouth. Then she dropped the bomb: "Dad, are you gay?"

I did not have to think before I pounced on her with a one-word answer: "No!"

She was not done. She followed up by asking, "How are you so sure?"

All I could say was, "Raka, baby, just know that I know."

The matter had gotten out of hand. I knew I stood no chance with regard to any future questions. But by that time, the captain had mercy on me. He announced that we were close to our final descent into Cincinnati. As we put our seat belts on, Raka was finally off the subject. Maybe she forgot, or maybe she had mercy on me after she realized how ignorant I was.

She was in a deep sleep with her hands around me as we landed.

~ In life there are two types of people. One asks questions and the other fails to answer the questions. ~

A RINGLEADER?
DENVER, COLORADO, 1998

I had just taken a job at Papa John's International in Louisville, Kentucky, and Raka was still in Colorado with her mother.

Once I got to Papa John's, the world of "Better Ingredients, Better Pizza" became real to me. I traveled to Modesto, California, to learn the story of the fresh, vine-ripened tomatoes used to make the pizza sauce. Soon I was learning about better mushrooms, better olives, and other chemical-free ingredients that are better for you.

Once I learned all this, there was one person I had to pass the learning to, Raka. When I came back to Denver over a weekend, Raka and I went to Papa John's to get a pizza. She was very excited to experience Dad's new work. We walked into the store, and she asked me if I would make the pizza for her. I explained to her that I worked in concept research and strategic planning in the corporate office. She looked at me. This was another instance in which Dad failed to answer the question.

She continued to look at me and said, "So you do not make pizza?"

"No, Raka, I do not make pizza," was my response.

Once we were sitting at the counter, enjoying the cheese sticks and cheese pizzas, I started telling Raka about my world at Papa John's. I told her about all the ingredient stories. She listened as amazement reflected in her eyes. When I was through, she asked me,

"But Dad, you worked for other pizza places before! So you mean that they are bad?"

I went on to explain to Raka in more detail about Papa John's ingredients and how the fresh ingredients made them a better pizza place. Raka was losing her interest in the conversation. Then she asked me, "Have you made any friends at Papa John's? Do you know John? Is he nice?" There were a lot of questions as we drove back home. After the weekend visit with Raka, I was back in Louisville Sunday evening.

That Tuesday I got a call from Denver—it was Ms. Terry from Raka's school. Ms. Terry was the owner of Garfield Montessori. This was the first time I had ever gotten a call from Raka's school. I knew these calls were never good. I asked Ms. Terry if everything was all right. She was in a serious mood and explained to me that Raka was fine and everything was okay in school other than …

"Yes, Ms. Terri, other than what?" I asked. I could not wait to hear what she had to say next.

"Mr. Sen," Ms. Terri continued, "every Tuesday we get pizza for lunch in school. As always, this week we have pizza from a local pizza place."

The mention of the word *pizza* gave me some idea of what was to come next, but I kept quiet and listened to Ms. Terry. She went on to say, "Today, when the pizza came in, Raka wanted to serve everyone because her father works at a pizza place. Then she looked at the pizza box and said that this was not good pizza. Initially, Mr. Sen, we did not take her seriously. Soon the staff realized that Raka was refusing to eat the pizza. As the staff started reasoning with Raka, Raka began convincing her classmates that they should not eat the pizza either. The staff then realized that they had a problem on their hands. Raka looked at everyone and said, 'My dad does not know how to make pizzas at Papa John's, but he knows that all other pizzas are bad for you.'"

So there was a dilemma at the school. The kids were refusing to eat their lunch, and the ringleader was my daughter. I asked to talk to Raka over the phone, and she was excited to talk to me. Before I could talk to her about the crisis at hand, Raka was asking me about John and other friends of mine in Louisville. Finally, I got to the point and explained to her that she should eat her lunch and have the pizza. I could sense Raka's utter surprise in her voice. "But Dad, you said that ..."

Finally, I reached a settlement with this tough negotiator. The kids would have cheese and crackers for lunch that day, and every Tuesday thereafter, Dad would arrange for Papa John's pizza for the school. I could live with that.

When I finally got off the phone, I could not believe Raka had taken me so seriously when I was talking to her about Papa John's. There I was, always wondering if she was actually listening to me.

~ Living what we say is the ultimate proof of belief. ~

A WEDDING IN THE FAMILY DENVER, COLORADO, 1999

It was one of those days that will always be in my memory. Raka was six years, three months, and nine days old. It was the shortest of special moments, but to me it was also the most special of all moments.

Raka was wearing a black dress; her hair was in a ponytail that stood up vertically on her head. She had that smile on. Audrey Hepburn must have looked like that when she was six. It was New Year's Eve, and as the evening progressed she came to me and gave me a huge hug. Then she said those five words that every dad dreams of hearing: "Dad, I want to marry you."

I was flattered, but my reactions were mixed. I wanted to say "awww," yet I also thought this could be one way of keeping boys away from her. I did not want to take her comment too seriously, but when she repeated her intent to marry me, I finally dared to ask the question, "Why get married? What happens after you get married?"

She looked at me with bright big eyes. She said, "You dance and eat ice cream."

I had a deal for her. I asked her if we could skip the marriage and get straight to ice cream and start dancing. She was happy. She agreed.

Somewhere in that enchanted evening, after a few dances and

ice cream, my princess bride was fast asleep on my shoulder. It was one of those moments. As I write about it I get teary eyed. I lifted her gently and carried her to bed. As I put her in bed and pulled the comforter over her, she opened her eyes wide and said, "I love you, Dad," and then she was out. Wow, what a wedding.

Today Raka is a young lady. When I remind her of that day, she tries to hide her blushing and pretends to act more mature than I. She gives me a hug and we skip the conversation and get right to ice cream.

~ When a princess offers you her hand, just take it. Those days do not come along in a frog's life too often. ~

TAKE-YOUR-DAUGHTER-TO WORK-DAY LOUISVILLE, KENTUCKY, 1999

Even though I was working hard at Papa John's, I was also trying very hard to be a good father. I had to do what good fathers do. A good father "brings" his daughter to work; he doesn't "take" her.

From time to time, when Raka had no school and I had to work, I would bring her to work with me. I would tell my assistant, Christy, a day ahead of time to make the place ready for Raka. At home the night before, Raka and I would go through what clothes she should wear. When we drove to work, I gave Raka clear instructions. When I think back, I had nearly prepared a training manual for her to survive the day at work. "You cannot talk loudly. You cannot bother any other employees. You cannot talk to me when I am on the phone or talking to others. You cannot go to the restroom alone. You cannot leave your space without my consent." There were a whole lot of cannots.

Christy would make room for Raka. Raka was placed in a space where she could do no damage with her own crayons, her own paper, and her own set of instructions. Lunch was always scheduled. How can a day at dad's work not include lunch? We would have lunch as two adults, but most of the time, my pager and my cell phone talked to me more than she did.

Even through all the rules, there she was, always smiling at me.

She was proud to be with her dad. She was soaking in every moment with me. She was happy. Somewhere in her smiles there was a hidden wisdom trying to show its face. Maybe she was trying to tell me that I needed to wake up. Maybe she was trying to tell me that I did not know what was slipping through my hands as we sat and ate lunch.

Today, when I think back, I feel ashamed at the drama. Why could I not create an environment for Raka to actually go to work? Why did I not give her a real opportunity to work? Why could I not trust her to do the right things?

It would not be until the summer of 2007 that I would realize what Raka was truly capable of. It would be in 2007 that I would realize what I missed on all those take-your-daughter-to-work days. Now that I realize what Raka is capable of, I know she would have presented me with more "wow" moments.

~ A child is never too young to be taken seriously. The same may not be true for a dad. ~

A DAY AT THE TRACK
LOUISVILLE, KENTUCKY, 2000

I was taking my team at Papa John's out for an off-site visit to Churchill Downs. It was not a major race day, but as a team we gathered and had some food, and a few of us bet on some of the races. Usually the bets were more for bragging rights than winning big.

As Raka did not have school that day, I brought her with me to the races. She was excited to go to the track to see horses, and when we all arrived, Raka became a favorite among my team. She vanished with my team while I spent time with various individuals, getting to know them personally outside the workplace.

Suddenly I heard something that I could not believe. Raka was surrounded by a few of my team members, who were involved in an intense conversation. When I approached, I learned that Raka was giving everyone tips on races. Initially I thought it was cute, but then I was told that Raka had predicted the winner in four of the last seven races; I had to take notice of the situation.

I walked over and took Raka to a corner. I wanted to know what she was doing. Even though I could not say it, I wanted to make sure that her smart tips were only for her father. She was excited when I wanted to know her secret. "How are you choosing the horses?" I asked.

Her answer was simply brilliant. "Dad, pink and purple cannot lose." They were her favorite colors.

We walked over and each got a Coke, and for the last race, I asked her which horse would win. She studied the names and the colors, and then she whispered something to me. I looked at the odds. The odds of that horse winning were fifty-five to one. I nodded my head and placed a ten-dollar bet. We walked down to the front to watch the race close up. The horses walked out and slowly headed toward the gate. We had our eyes on Raka's horse. I could not believe that I, too, was loudly cheering for that horse to win. Raka's wisdom had taken over my senses. Raka was holding my hand tightly in excitement as the race began. She was screaming at the top of her little lungs.

The race ended, and Raka's horse came in second. She was very happy for her horse. Then she looked at me and asked, "What did we win, Dad?"

I told her, "A whole lot of Barbie dolls."

On the way home we stopped at Target, and Raka got her Barbie dolls.

~ For every question, there is a simple answer that will set you free. As we grow older, the answer leaves us. ~

SOCCER COACHING
LOUISVILLE, KENTUCKY, 2000

Monsoon season in Kolkata meant the fields would be waterlogged, but the rules were simple. No amount of rain could stop a soccer match when we were on the field. I even remember squeezing in games of soccer during lunch hours at school. The teachers would not allow us to come back to class with muddy, spoiled clothes, so we found a simple solution: we would take our shirts and pants off and wear them inside out during soccer. After the game, we reversed them again before we headed back to class—simple, yet remarkable.

Raka got her share of soccer genes from me. When she wanted to start soccer, I quickly consented to be the coach. Every Wednesday evening we had practice and every Saturday we had a game. Christy, being a good assistant at work, put Raka's soccer schedule on my calendar with a thirty-minute pre-event reminder. Then the games started.

I was a good coach, not because I was professionally trained to teach soccer, but because I did not care about winning. What I wanted most was for each child on my team to create a memory. The youngest girl on the team badly wanted to score a goal. During scrimmage, I would play against the rest of the team with her on my side. One day I passed the ball to her in front of the goal and she scored. I cannot forget how elated she was. She ran to me and jumped on my lap. I have not seen this level of excitement in any U.S. women's soccer star, ever.

We could have won a lot of matches. I had a few star players on my team, and if I played my stars and rotated the rest in, wins were guaranteed. Instead, I decided to rotate all the players so each player got an equal chance. Every parent knew that, and they supported my focus on equality and not on winning. Coaching the team was an ordeal. I ran up and down the sideline screaming, "Kick! Run! Kick!" The kids always reacted to me as I stood behind the goalie and screamed, "Move left, right; now grab the ball." If I did not direct at the right time, the goalie would be late in grabbing the ball, the ball would wind up inside the net, and then of course the goalie would look at me and remind me it was my fault.

There was one event that put all this into perspective. I was away on business during one match and put two other parents in charge of the team. The team was having a bad day. Raka was the goalkeeper and had conceded five goals. Her mom was there and was getting restless seeing Raka "fail" to stop a single goal. Finally she did the unthinkable. She screamed at Raka. The rest of the parents could not believe what had just happened. Raka was in tears. Before the rest of the parents could react, before Raka's tears were dry, Raka walked up to her mom. She looked straight up at her and said, "Mom, this is not the Olympics. The Olympics are happening on TV. This is Dad's team. Dad does not scold anyone for not winning. Can you go to the car and wait?"

When I came back the following week, each parent told me the story. I was proud of Raka and amazed at her level of maturity, but I had no idea what was awaiting me next on the soccer field.

~ It is about having fun. A true genius forgets the game at hand and can enjoy the wildflower coming out of the grass. ~

END OF SOCCER
LOUISVILLE, KENTUCKY, 2001

It was the last game of soccer Raka ever played. My brother, who was visiting from India, was at the game. Of course, at the beginning of the game, I had no idea that she would never want to play soccer after that day.

The match started, and one of my boys was moving with the ball from the left wing. He dribbled past one player and pushed the ball to the center of the box. Raka was running in from the center and was there at the top of the box exactly when the ball arrived. I had taught my team to always stop the ball and then kick. On this instance, Raka did not do that. She just kicked the ball coming from her left. She connected perfectly, and the ball flew past the goal keeper, all the way into the top corner of the net.

A stunning pass, an equally stunning shot; what a goal! The Brazilians would have broken into a samba near the corner flag after such a goal. For me, the euphoria did not last long, as Raka came to me and said, "I am done, Dad." I asked her to take a seat. She walked up to me and said, "Dad, you do not get it, do you? I am done, done. I am not playing soccer any more. I am done."

As we drove home after the game, I asked Raka to explain to me what had happened. Raka told me she did not enjoy sweaty stuff. Soccer was too sweaty for her preference. I asked her, "If you do not like sweaty stuff, then why did you even start soccer?"

Her answer came without any thinking, "Because I can spend time with my daddy. I love that."

I just could not believe what I had heard. My little girl had picked up a sport I loved just so she could spend more time with me? Wow! That was beyond my comprehension.

Even though Raka said that she was done with soccer, I was not done with soccer. I asked her again that same evening, "Raka, is soccer not fun for you anymore? Are you sure you want to quit?"

Raka was busy getting ready to practice a dance with my brother. She gave me a sidelong glance and said, "No, it was not fun."

As I talked to her, I learned she had no time to play or have fun. Her life after school was on a tight routine. Monday piano, Tuesday and Thursday swimming, Wednesday and Saturday soccer, and dance on Friday and Sunday. Somehow, on her schedule, there was no room for play. There was no room for fun. When would she play?

I recalled my days of consenting, and I thought maybe Raka, too, was becoming addicted to consenting. My theory on consenting was short-lived, though, when Raka explained the answer to me. "Dad, you like soccer, and therefore I played soccer. Mom likes to dance, and therefore I danced." I did not need her to finish the thought. I got it. I guess I was reliving my soccer days through her.

It was one of the times Raka's mom and I listened to her. Her schedule would change to only include things she wanted to do. Soccer was gone. Raka was in touch with her own life.

~ Attention all parents. Stop living your lives through your children. Let them have fun. ~

2001 TO 2007

DAY AFTER SEPTEMBER 11

I was holding the piece of paper with Raka's three questions:

1. Who is my best friend?
2. What is my favorite restaurant?
3. What is the best thing you and I have ever done?

I failed to answer any of the three questions correctly. On top of it all, I tried to lie and get myself out of the mess. Raka saw right through my lies and said, "Dad, I love you. So you do not have to lie to me. I want to go to Denver, you know that, but if you really wanted to go to Denver, by now we would have gone back."

I was embarrassed, I was humiliated. On top of it all, I was ashamed of who I had become. What should I do next? I did not know. Do I ignore the discussion, and go back to doing what I was doing, or do I take this wake-up call seriously?

That night, I was bent on changing all that. I was bent on proving to Raka that I was not lying to her anymore. I was determined to prove to her that I was worthy of her love. That night the answer came to me. Yes, I would leave everything and go back to Denver with Raka. I would learn everything she liked to do. I would prepare myself for the next quiz, and that would be all that mattered in my life. I was ready to wake up. I felt good about the new energy in me, but I was scared, very scared.

What happened in the next few days can at best be called a CLM, a career limiting move. I ended my professional connections with my company, and once everything was taken care of, I told Raka that I would work from home. I would be there for her more, to take her to school and bring her back, and I would now seriously try to move us back to Denver. There was light in her eyes as she gave me a long hug.

Unlike the previous conversation, I think this time she believed me, but I took no chances. I showed her my severance documents, and she actually read them. I was not a liar anymore in her eyes, and that was all I needed. A lost dad needed a little reassurance to find his way back home, and I knew I was on the right track. After I saw the light in her eyes, I could never get lost again. The journey home had begun.

My life thus far has been full of wake-up calls. Some of the wake-up calls have been figurative, some literal. Some have been loud, some prolonged. There have been times I woke up after a wake-up call, and there have been times I snoozed. Every wake-up call in my life, figurative or literal, has had a purpose, and it has always been up to me to figure that purpose out. This wake-up call woke me up for good. There was no more going back.

~ The biggest challenge after a wake-up call is to take the first step. The rest simply happens. ~

BABY STEPS
DENVER, COLORADO, 2001

As I quit the corporate world to start my own consulting business, life changed completely. I had all the time in the world. Earlier, my life was booked solid—it was tough to add an event to it at the last minute. Now the pace of life had changed. I woke up, made breakfast for Raka, and took her to school. When I got back home, I made a few calls; the rest of my professional day consisted of waiting for the phone to ring.

I knew the timing of every show on the game show network. I was getting quite good at guessing the prices on *The Price is Right*. The next major event of the day was waiting for the mail carrier; she usually came at 1:30. Over time I realized she liked Diet Pepsi, so I would sit outside with a Diet Pepsi, waiting for the mail carrier to arrive. If she was late, it would worry me.

The next event of the day was Raka coming back from school. She would look at me and ask, "How was your day?" Then she would start sharing her day. "Guess what, Daddy ..." The first fifteen minutes after she got back from school were when she opened her life's book. She wanted to share everything about her day with me.

This reminded me of the days when I was her age. It was a five-minute walk from the school bus stop to home, and when I walked through my front door and threw my school bag on the floor, I would rush to the kitchen. There was my grandmother, my Maiji. She had food ready for me. On a summer day, it was yogurt, rice, and mango all blended together in a way only she could blend it. Or she would make a wrap with leftover homemade tortillas and curries. As I ate, she would go through my bag and take my lunch box out. We would talk about school, my friends, my day, and my homework.

As I watched Raka, excited after she got back from school, I was taken back to my childhood days. I had forgotten how Maiji was there for me every day, every moment, and I was glad Raka was getting me there, slowly.

While I indulged in my nostalgia, Raka would ask me, "Dad, how was your day? Anyone call you? Did you get any work?" I would just look at her, and she would know that I had nothing to report.

The early days of consulting were tough. There were no projects. The only people who contacted were those who wanted to pick my brain for free. I was not even getting the chance to fail. No one would talk to me; I had no chance to even show what I could do.

I was hopeful. I was determined. Watching Raka from close up made the time at home worth it.

~ The rewards of life do not always come in conventional forms. ~

THE FIRST BOARD MEETING
DENVER, COLORADO, 2002

As the days passed, Raka got more involved in the business. She asked more detailed questions, and her seriousness was contagious. Just when I was close to losing hope, she would energize me to recommit to this new adventure.

Over time, we started talking in a more structured way when she got back from school. One day I talked to her about the fact that I had incorporated the business. She was happy and told me that we were officially a big company. Then she asked me, "Dad, how are you spending money in the company when you are not making any money?" Very interesting question. I explained to her the concept of investors, shareholders, and boards.

The next afternoon, the board of our company was formed. Raka and I were in.

During the first board meeting, Raka was learning about investors and other concepts when she got up and walked away. She came back with four quarters she wanted to invest in the business. It was everything she had. She was investing partially because she believed in the business, but more because she believed in her dad. I was proud and was determined not to disappoint.

Over the years, she has been paid rich dividends for her investment. Returns have come in the form of Nintendo games, clothes, movies, and more. (She is not much into cash dividends.) A few years later, when the business was doing well, a friend of ours wanted to buy out her share. Raka thought for a while, because it was her business, too, and politely declined.

I was always excited about our board meetings. I would prepare an agenda and summarize my day's activities. This was a serious professional reality for me. Raka would listen and ask questions, and then she always would say, "Dad, great job." I needed those compliments.

One day when she got back from school, I was watching TV. It was 3:45 PM. Raka looked at me and I knew I was in trouble. When we had our meeting that day she said that she was disappointed in my actions for watching TV during work. This is the same kid who taught me that I could not call her bad, mean, or any other names. She is always good. I can, of course, call some of her actions bad, mean, or other names. Today she was doing exactly that to me. I tried to defend myself. Then she said, "If you were working for Papa John's, would you watch TV at 3:45?" Before I could answer, she asked again, "Would you allow our employees in this company to watch TV during work?" Of course she was right.

Life changed after that. When I was bored in the afternoons and watched TV, I would turn it off right before she came home. One afternoon after she got home, she had a strange look. She was planning to go out and play with the neighbor's kids, but instead she walked to the TV and put her hand on top. It was still warm. Someone had left evidence at the crime scene. That day I was strongly reprimanded in the board meeting. "Not only are you breaking the board's rules, now you are lying?" Very serious charges were brought against me. I am glad she loved me enough to let me off the hook. I survived that meeting.

As my consulting career evolved, there were quite a few temptations to return to the corporate world. Attractive titles and decent compensation packages at great companies were lining up. Early in my consulting days, I found it tough to say no to these offers, but they were getting easier to turn down. In one case, I simply stated that I would take the job if I could:

1. Work from home
2. Take off anytime I wanted, without being questioned

3. Never be fired

The reason I could ask for this is because it is exactly what my current consulting job allows me. I can be there with my daughter anytime she needs me, and anytime I want.

~ It is tough to find the right path. It is equally tough to stay on the path once you have found it. ~

THE ELEPHANT GOD
DENVER, COLORADO, 2002

Earlier, I mentioned the Bengali Indian families in Colorado and their behavior when they gather for a religious meeting. Durga Puja is one of their biggest religious events, celebrated over three days. Here in Colorado, all the families originally from Bengal, India, gather together. The day starts with a modified religious ceremony with a representation of the goddess on a stage. As the day goes on, the whole event turns into a festival in which women showcase their new saris and jewelry, kids run around and play, and men sit in a corner, play cards, and await a big feast.

One of the last times I was there, I felt sad as I realized what these kids were missing. They had no Maiji to tell them stories about Indian mythology. Their lives would evolve with the knowledge gained from books, and not from word of mouth.

So for the next religious festival, I decided to make a presentation on the mythological stories related to the celebration. The research part was easy as I went through some of the books Maiji had marked, as well as some research on the internet. Once the research was done, I felt it would be amazing if the kids could tell the stories to the group instead of me. I chose a few kids to tell stories, and I asked Raka to tell the story of Lord Ganesha, the elephant god.

Practice started right away, and I soon realized how serious the kids were about these stories. Raka rehearsed with me every day; she wanted to tell the story right.

On the day of the festival, Raka was wearing a red sari. When her turn came, she started her story of why Lord Ganesha has one broken tusk and why he wears a snake for a belt. I stood next to the stage and watched Raka tell the story in the way only Raka can. She started with her typical statement, "Do you know ...?" As she went through the story, I stood in disbelief. Simply amazing. The only other person I had seen tell a story so well was Maiji. I knew that wherever she was, she was proud of her great-granddaughter, telling the story to other kids, spreading the word around.

*~ If you open the door, people will show you
how good they can be. ~*

DIRECT MAIL CAMPAIGN DENVER, COLORADO, 2003

I was still trying to establish the consulting business when we moved to Colorado. Every day, Raka would ask me if I had any work, and every day my answer was the same: "I am working on a few things and something will happen soon."

Raka would then look at me and say, "Hmm, that means you have no work?"

As adults, we do not like to make direct confessions of our failure. So, I would respond with a long answer on the concept of the pipeline of projects and the patience needed to build a business. In one such effort, I bought a list from the Colorado Restaurant Association. It was a "very active" list of potential clients in the field who were in the area.

I told Raka that we would market the business using this list, and she was excited. I took the list and converted it into address labels, and when each address label was printed and ready, I developed a postcard describing the business. Raka and I proofed it and sent it to the printer. Next, both of us went to the post office to choose the right stamp. She thoughtfully considered her options before she decided on the right stamp.

Now we were ready to launch. The postcards were back from the printer, and the stamps and address labels were ready to go. Raka sat and meticulously put the labels and stamps in place to get them ready for their outward journey. I was simply amazed by her attention to detail. She made sure that every label and every stamp was placed in its proper place, straight. Her reason was simple. We were sending out a lot of cards, but each client would get only one. Based on the one postcard, the potential client would decide whether to work with us or not.

I am not completely sure of the exact number of mailings we sent out, but I estimate the number to be close to 2000. When I tucked Raka into bed that night, she could not hide her excitement. She was sure that the next day we would get a lot of calls and e-mails. Soon we would be flooded with work. Then what would happen? My princess went to sleep thinking about that.

The next day, Raka came back from school and ran to me. "Dad, Dad! How many people called?"

I could not look at her as I said, "None, baby."

She went to the mailbox to see twenty returned cards, the addresses not deliverable. She wanted me to call the Colorado Restaurant Association and complain. After that, each night before she went to bed she consoled me and said, "Dad, do not worry. Tomorrow is a big day. Tomorrow they will call."

Tomorrow never came. Every day the story was the same. Raka would pick up the returned postcards and stack them together. Slowly she stopped asking me the question. She already knew the answer by the look on my face.

Finally, one day, she asked me a profound question, "Dad, if you cannot market your own business, how can you market other companies?"

Good question, Raka. Let us not share this with our clients.

~ Sharing your failures will bring you closer. ~

A GUEST IN THE CLASSROOM
DENVER, COLORADO, 2004

Those days I was teaching at the University of Colorado at Boulder. I started the assignment because there was mutual need: I was in need of cash (as my consulting business had yet to take off), and the school had a last-minute opening. I was the best available candidate, and I got the job.

On the first day, I realized I had close to five hundred students in each section. As I delivered my lecture, I felt like a preacher who was simply doing his duty by delivering a message. The students were in and out of the class like a herd, but once I got to know each of them, I started seeing the excitement in their eyes. Office hours were fascinating. Students would come in, some more lost than others. I remember some distinct conversations.

One particular girl came in, sat down, and began talking about her quarter-life crisis. As I listened to her, I saw my own midlife crisis in the rearview mirror of my life. Then I tried to think of my quarter-life crisis. Did I ever have it? What happened during it? Finally, I resigned myself to the fact that I was too old to recollect.

Students came in to discuss their inventions and products that would solve the world's problems. Then there were the parents who would visit the campus and come in to meet the faculty. All these interactions were getting me to like teaching even more. I was learning from my students every day.

In an effort to help my students market themselves better, I started reviewing their résumés. I realized the void in the job done by career services on campus. They looked at each student's résumé and then gave them some "good examples," which they asked the students to follow. In short, they encouraged all the students to conform. If I were to extend the vision of career services, all business students would be wearing the same uniforms and feature the same distinctive haircuts. They would walk the same way, and talk the same way. In my humble opinion, this is wrong. Student need to be encouraged to accept the fact that each of them is different. The question that they need to address is how they can develop a relevant, marketable differentiator that makes them special. Conforming may be the safe answer, but it is never the right answer. Growing up as a champion conformer, I was sure of this.

As I talked to my students, my mind drifted back to the days when I applied for my first job after graduation. My resume was on a red piece of paper. It was a film strip. At the time, Nike ran an ad featuring Bo Jackson called "Bo Knows." My résumé said in each of the strips of the film, "Arjun knows" this, "Arjun knows" that, and finally, "can Bo do this"?

To me it was brilliant. It had my Arjun-ness signature all over the strange résumé. It felt like Michael Jordan in the air, dunking the ball with his signature tongue out. I sent the résumé to two places: Pizza Hut corporate and IBM. Pizza Hut immediately called me and I got an offer. I guess they loved the creative energy they saw in me. I never heard back from IBM. Four months later, I called IBM. When I enquired about my résumé, I realized that I was quite famous in IBM too. The person in human resources informed me that it had taken IBM years to evolve from plain white shirts to vertical stripes. My résumé was a few hundred years ahead of its time.

As I got settled in at CU Boulder, I started to venture out and ask my students questions. Before class I would walk around and interact with the energetic students in the class. The energy in the classroom changed completely after that.

One day, during her spring break, Raka came to my class. Raka was already famous in class because I told a lot of Raka stories to illustrate marketing principles. I always referred to Raka's story about refusing to eat anything other than Papa John's pizza as an example of brand insistence. In short, *The Famous Raka* was in class that day.

She sat in the front row as I led a discussion. All of a sudden I realized that all my students were looking at the front of the classroom, but not toward me. One little hand was raised. Raka had a question. I signaled to her with my eyes that this was not the right time, and we would talk later. I knew her well enough now to know that I never had good answers to her questions. Raka kept her hand up for a few minutes then took it down. She never got a chance to ask her question, but she started scribbling down something. I knew I may have dodged a public bullet, but she was not going to let it pass.

On the way back, Raka read me her question. In class, I talked about brands like Xerox which become so strong that they developed into generic verbs like "Xeroxing" instead of copying or duplicating. In my opinion, brands have to own a category, without becoming generic, and must strike the perfect balance. Raka was sitting in the backseat as she explained to me that I was wrong on this. She explained how Kleenex is the name of the category and it makes her realize that if a box of tissues does not have the name Kleenex, it is a bad box. Band-Aid was her next example. I knew she was right. I also knew I was right in not admitting that she was right, as I would then never hear the end of that conversation. I just said a meaningful "hmm" at the end of her comments.

Raka came to class with me often after that day. Before and after class, she always mingled with my students. As I stared at Raka, she gave me a new perspective on my students. These were all kids only 50 percent older than Raka, and soon my daughter would arrive at their age. This realization helped me interact with my students more tenderly and with more gentle kindness and patience. This lesson helped me offer a make-up exam to a student who missed the regular exam but was honest enough to admit that the party the night before was to blame.

Marketing was just a path these kids chose as they moved forward in life. Life was more than marketing.

~ A teacher learns more from a classroom than any student learns from the teacher. ~

OUTER CIRCLE
DENVER, COLORADO, 2003

I will always admit that I am a dad-in-training. I never would brag about being a perfect dad, but with my little coach guiding me, I also felt I was not that bad. However, one Saturday morning in September 2003 really hit me hard. I hesitated quite a few times before I decided to share this particular story, but as it contains one of the bigger lessons for me, I feel I must.

It was a relaxed Saturday morning. Raka had just woken up, and after we had a simple breakfast, we planned to ride our bikes over to visit one of my friends in the neighborhood. We got our helmets and our bottled water and were all set to go out. Before we left, Raka went up to her room and came down with a piece of paper. She thought for a while and then decided to show it to me.

I had no clue what was on the paper. When she brought the paper close to me, I saw a series of concentric circles drawn on the paper. I thought it might be some kind of target practice. I still did not have a clue on what was on the paper.

Finally Raka explained the diagrams. "Dad, do you see all the circles?" I nodded. Raka went on to explain, "Dad, do you see this circle in the middle, the smallest of circles?" She was referring to the innermost circle. "That circle is where I am. Based on how close people are to me, they are in different circles. Those closest to me are in the circles next to me." She took a long breath, and then she went on, "My mom is in the first circle, the same as me. Rollie (Raka's dog) is also in that circle."

I was now anxious to know my grade; I wanted to know where I stood. I had a strange feeling that this may not be a good report card. I did not need to ask. Raka told me that I was on the eighth circle, the furthest from her. I looked at the paper closely to see if there was any way this could be a good thing. Unfortunately, there was no good news in all this. So, I just thanked her for sharing this with me. I did not know what else there was to say.

The whole day passed slowly and gloomily. It was tough to stare at reality as seen by my own little daughter. That night, when she went to bed, I stared at the paper. Tears started coming down my cheeks. I did not know what to do. I was very lost.

That night seemed extra long. I could not sleep—I was thinking. Finally, I had my answer. I felt good, finally, after I had my answer. I went to bed.

The next morning, as I drove Raka to her mom's house, I decided to talk about the subject of the circles. Raka was sitting next to me, with Rollie on her lap. I told her, "Raka, I do not know if I wanted you to share the circles diagram with me. I was hurt to know that I am in the eighth circle, and furthest from you. But, you know what, baby?" This got Raka's attention. She looked at me with her bright eyes, anxious to know what I would say next. "Baby, I thought a lot last night. I realized that I just want to be me and be the best dad I can be to you. I cannot do anything different based on where I am on the circles. I am not going to try to move closer to you. I just love you and will continue to love you."

Raka nodded her head. I was not sure that what I wanted to say was getting through to her. Being an adult, I wanted to emphasize and restate what I was telling her. "Baby, I love you. Whether you love me or not, or if you do not feel close to me, I cannot love you any less. All I know is that every day I love you more."

I would have gone on for a third round of speeches, but Raka cut me short. "Baba, I love you. Can we stop for somewhere for some ice cream please?"

I agreed. I also realized that I had spoken too much, and there was no need to beat a dead horse. I felt good about the conversation.

~ Some roles in life and some actions are not transactional. Just doing your best job is good enough. ~

THE CURSE OF TWO HOUSES
DENVER, COLORADO, 2004

It is the American dream to own your own home. Owning two homes is typically a sign of affluence, but can owning two homes ever become a curse? In 2003, when Raka's mom and I finalized our divorce, Raka inherited this curse.

Raka has two homes. She is with me at our home for half the time and with her mom at her mom's house half the time. The houses are a mile apart, and traveling from house to house is not difficult. In the summertime, Raka even rides her bike from one house to the other.

As Raka's school activities got more and more intense, Raka would often remember something she had left at her mother's place. It was quite tiring to drive Raka to her mom's place, late at night, to get that one thing she had forgotten. It got even worse when right after we got back from her mom's place, we realized she had forgotten something else.

This situation of moving back and forth really hit home one snowy evening. The roads were messy, and at 9:30 PM Raka realized she needed to get her books from her mom's place. I warmed the car and took Raka over. I waited in the car while Raka went inside. Raka came back after ten minutes with her books, and we drove back home. Within minutes of reaching home, Raka came and knocked on my bedroom door. Her face told the story.

"Dad, we have a problem," she uttered. I did not like the sound of it. I stared at the television and asked her what the problem was. "Dad, I need to go back to my mom's place. I need to get my shoes." I could not believe it. I screamed at her and expressed that there was no way I was going out again this late.

Raka did not leave. She stood there. Even though she was determined, I saw a sense of helplessness in her eyes. I guess she could not get her shoes without my help.

I got up, got dressed, walked down the stairs, and got in the car. Raka was next to me, quiet. I gave her an earful about this kind of disorganized behavior. Raka was still quiet. We stopped at her mom's place, where Raka dashed in and quickly came back out with her shoes.

On the way back, I went on expressing my displeasure with her. We got home and locked the door. As Raka went upstairs to her room, I could not resist an outburst, reminding Raka that she was old enough to act responsibly.

Raka stopped. This time she looked up and had her eyes fixed on me. "Dad, you realize that I did not choose to live in the two houses. Have you ever realized what it feels like to live like that? I do not even take my toothbrush from one house to the other." Wow. I had never thought about it that way.

That night as I went to bed, I realized the significance of what she had said. I realized how helpless she was and what a very tough price she pays for her parents' divorce. I realized how occasionally on business trips I forget to take quite a few things with me. I could understand Raka's plight. It was sad. I felt ashamed to have scolded her.

During breakfast the next morning, I was ready for an uncomfortable conversation. This was not the first time I would tell Raka I was wrong. This was not the first time she knew I was wrong. This was also not the first time she would say, "That is okay, Dad," then leave me with a hug. So why delay the inevitable?

As Raka walked down the stairs, I was ready, but I did not know where to start. I started by saying, "I am sorry, baby." She was busy getting her books in her bag and making sure she had everything she needed. She looked at me with still-sleepy eyes. I continued, "I am sorry, baby. Before we talked last night, I never realized that this divorce affects you every day."

Raka gave me a swift hug and started moving her bag into the car.

As I dropped her off at school that day and watched her walk away from the car, I felt bad about her plight. I promised myself that I would never ever give her grief for making me make these extra trips between her two homes. It is not easy for her. It was not meant to be this way, baby.

~ People should not be punished for things they did not do.
Listening is important, and creating an environment for listening is
even more important. ~

WAKE UP, RAKA!
DENVER, COLORADO, 2006

When Raka was thirteen, she had to be at school by 7:40 AM, so I woke her up at 6:50 each morning she was with me. I really looked forward to her first innocent smile of the day. My little baby!

Every morning, the routine was the same. After I woke her up, I would go downstairs to make breakfast, and then I would anxiously await the appearance of my princess. At 7:10, I would start to get restless. By 7:15, I knew that she was running late and I would let out a loud scream from the kitchen, "*Raakkkkkkkuu!* You are going to be late!!!"

I was sure that there was nothing at all wrong with occasional screaming. Most parents will be siding with me, as we all feel that kids need a major wake-up call when they are late. One morning, Raka was going extra slow, so of course my scream that day was extra loud. I was freaking out. How could my daughter be so tardy? Raka slowly came down, grabbed her breakfast to go, and we were off to school. As we drove, she looked at me from the passenger seat and said, "Dad, why do you scream at me? Do you realize that some days, it takes me extra time to wake up? Do you realize that when you scream, you simply rattle me? It scares me. After that, it takes me a while to get back into life at school."

I was totally confused. What was she talking about? Rattling her with my screaming? I was trying to make some sense of all this when we pulled into her school. Raka got her belongings, reached out and kissed me, and then walked to the main entrance of her school.

As I left the school parking lot, I kept pondering. Wow, a small scream does that to a person? When I was in the corporate world, I was used to throwing my weight around to get things done. Hmm, that must not have been a good management system if my screaming negatively impacted people the same way at work.

The next morning, I was a changed man. I softly knocked on her door to wake her up. Then I gently entered her room and touched her hand to wake her up. I waited till she gave me a hand signal that she was awake. Before I left her room to go down and start on breakfast, I paused at the door and looked at her still in bed, covered with numerous pillows and blankets. I stared at her and wondered what more in life I would learn from this kid.

~ A strong message does not need to be accompanied by a strong tone. ~

SUMMER OF '06: INTERNATIONAL DEBUT DENVER, COLORADO, 2006

Raka and I had a plan to beat jet lag on our long flight from Denver to Mumbai, India. We were both planning to stay awake all through the flight so that when we got to Mumbai, we would fall asleep at the local night time.

It was an eight-hour flight. I was falling asleep after the first few hours, but Raka was strict and would not let me sleep. We played games and watched movies. Raka had succeeded in keeping me awake for the first six hours of the flight from Mumbai to London, but finally her little eyes could take no more. She reached out and held my hand and vanished into the deepest of deep sleeps. Her tiny head rested peacefully on my shoulder. It was one of those moments I have learned to live for. I would not move to simply hear her breathe next to me. My little baby had grown so big, yet she was still my little baby.

As always, Raka would toss and turn in her sleep and even mumble a few words from time to time. In her early childhood, she would even eat in her dreams or play some sports. On this day, as she moved in her sleep, I did not even realize that she had stopped holding my hand until she turned over to grab the hand of the man in the seat on the other side of her. The man was startled. I was embarrassed and tried to reach out and pull Raka's hands off, but the kind gentleman hinted at me to not wake up the little darling. I complied for a few seconds and then gently pulled Raka's hands off the gentleman's hands and put them back on mine. I guess I took the first step in declaring that I would find it very tough to accept the day she reaches for the hand of a man other than her dad.

When we arrived in Mumbai, we were hit with the Agni hurricane. Agni is my nephew, then three months old. From the first moment, Raka and Agni connected. The next few days were spent with both Raka and me waking up with Agni, eating with Agni, and napping around Agni on his bed as he napped. Raka was the big sister who would not leave Agni out of her sight, even for a second. There was magic in the air.

Then came the most magical moment of all. My brother Oni, an ad filmmaker, was working on an ad for a hand cream. Raka always liked to hang out with Oni Kaka and decided to join him as an intern on the sets. I could not believe the seriousness in Raka's eyes as she walked on to the sets with Oni.

Soon Raka was best friends with Gopal Sir, a renowned cinematographer. Gopal Sir and Raka would talk about different shots as Raka watched what Oni was doing closely. Next came the debut moment. The crew needed a finger model to display the hand lotion. Who better than Raka? Of course my brother would never be biased in selecting Raka for such an important job. Raka got a quick manicure and was ready for the camera. My daughter was an international finger model! Wow! I could not believe it. Of course I stared at my fingers to see if she got it from her dad.

The day after filming the TV commercial, the crew was planning to do an overnight shoot at a mall after it closed. Raka scoped out the project with my brother and then expressed her desire to work all night. Initially I was taken aback, and the answer was a definite no. But since my brother, too, was batting hard for Raka, I decided to listen to their logic. For Raka, it was the chance of a lifetime to work with Oni. Oni convinced me that Raka would be taken care of, and if she got tired, a car would bring her back to me immediately.

I consented, and Raka gave me a hug in reward. I always prefer the normal, day-to-day hugs over these reward hugs. Somehow these hugs have the phrase "I got you, Dad" written all over them. Raka then rushed away to prepare her survival kit for the night and was off to shoot with my brother.

I was not there for the shoot, but early the next morning, Raka returned, tired. She went off to bed immediately and was asleep for nearly twenty hours, recovering from her first night shift. When I talked to my brother and his team, I was impressed with their tales of Raka's accomplishments. Raka was on her toes all night, working hard to assist the team. She did not complain even once. She ate with the crew and was the darling of the team, even before the night shift was over.

~ The timing for when a little bird is ready to fly is determined by her own confidence, not her father's comfort level. ~

THE GOOD SAMARITAN
LONDON, UNITED KINGDOM, 2007

After an eventful India trip, Raka and I were on our way back to Denver. It was the same route. First we flew from Mumbai to London, and then we took another long flight from London to Denver. Between flights, we had a six-hour layover in London, so Raka and I checked into one of the waiting lounges. We napped a little, ate some munchies, and watched TV.

An hour before our departure, we freshened up and left the lounge. As we walked slowly to our gate, I found it tough to follow the British accent of the announcers. Just as we neared our gate, Raka pointed out that British Airways was announcing a gate change for our flight. I do not remember the exact change, but I do remember that we had a very short time to go a very long distance.

We were rushing and Raka was leading the charge. All of a sudden, an elderly woman coming toward us bumped into a fellow passenger. She had a bag full of duty-free goodies that flew everywhere. Most of the goodies were recoverable, but her box of candies opened up and they flew all around. I felt bad. Here was this old lady who must have bought these candies for a near and dear one, maybe grandkids, and everyone was too busy walking to their destination to stop and help. However, everyone made sure they gave the old lady some space to pick up her candies.

I was back in my rush-to-catch-our-flight mode when I realized that Raka had walked away from me and gone toward the old lady. She was on the floor, picking up the candies and helped the lady pack all her goodies together. The old lady was of course relieved and happy. At the end, she offered Raka some candies. Raka smiled and refused as she said, "They are not mine."

The next instant she dashed back to me, held my hand, and started dragging me toward the gate. "Dad, come on. We are going to be late."

I did not care about the flight anymore. I was soaking in the goodness of my daughter.

~ There is one right thing to do. Even watching someone else do it when we fail to do it ourselves allows all to bask in that person's goodness. ~

THE FIRST PRESENTATION
DENVER, COLORADO, 2007

Our consulting business was starting to look good. We had a few clients, a few projects, and Raka was always there to show her interest and encourage me. If she had no school, I would take her with me to client locations.

One day, Raka was with me at a client site. It was a very informal meeting as the client happened to be my friend Trey. Raka had known Trey all her life and really liked him and his wife, Ann. That day, I was busy wrapping up a presentation while Raka sat in an empty cubicle on her own. She was bored.

After a while she came to me and asked, "Dad, can I do anything to help you?"

I told her, "Not yet, baby. I will need another thirty minutes to finish the presentation, and then you can review it and give me your feedback." Raka was very good in proofing and reviewing a presentation. She tried hard to understand the concepts behind a presentation, and her questions and insights were always relevant. I had learned to take her opinion seriously.

She went back to her cube, then returned in a few minutes and asked, "Can I do a presentation on my own?"

"Of course, baby," I said as I looked up from the laptop. "What do you need for your presentation?"

She began to raid my box of crayons and colored pencils for the appropriate supplies. She had a big smile on as she walked back to her cube with some colored pencils and paper.

My mind left my presentation as I saw her vanish into her cube. I realized again how fortunate I was. I had my princess with me while I was at work. I had another thirty to forty-five minutes of work to do, and then we would have lunch and go to the movies. Wow! All this on a Wednesday? Life could not get any better than this.

I was starting to get carried away with my thoughts when I looked at the time. I had twenty-five minutes left. I dove back into the world of PowerPoint and got busy finalizing the presentation.

After I finished, I realized Raka was also done with her presentation. She had her work on a few 11x17 sheets of paper, carefully folded to preserve the element of surprise. As we waited for Trey, Raka went through my presentation and started asking questions. We were discussing the content when Trey called me into his office. I walked in with Raka and started my quick presentation. It was well received. Even though I was serious about my work, a part of my mind was thinking about the date Raka and I had planned after this.

After my presentation, Raka told Trey that she had a different presentation for him. Trey had a look at his calendar and then asked Raka and me to stay in his office. Raka started her presentation. She was amazing. The confidence, the articulate words, and the simplicity all made it worth watching. Trey was pleasantly surprised and asked Raka if she could make the presentation to his entire team. Raka was ready.

More accolades. More praises. A proud dad watched it again from his courtside seat. Raka was a happy girl. After a quick lunch, we were off the movies.

Now I think back and compare this day to my earlier take-your-daughter-to-work days. It was now, truly, Raka's day. She had every reason to look forward to it, as she was now doing more than just coming along. I trusted her. There was no need to tell her how to dress or what to do. Because of my trust, she too would hold herself to higher standards. She always acted as an accompanying work colleague.

And we were experiencing all this in our own company! Wow!

It was one of those moments when I was truly proud of myself.

Arjun Sen

I had learned my lessons and was reaping the rewards of my better actions. But then again, my princess had held my hand to get me there. All credit goes to her. I was simply following her with an enchanted daze on my face.

~ Learning is simply priceless. After you learn, it is entertaining to look back at past mistakes. ~

SUMMER OF 2007

THE *START* OF A PRESIDENCY
DENVER, COLORADO, 2007

For the summer of 2007, I wanted to do something different. I was tired of Raka waking up and saying she had nothing to do, a typical problem faced by parents of teenagers. I decided to help Raka set up the teen division of our company, Restaurant Marketing Group. My objectives were simple. Raka would stay engaged, she would be home with some of her friends, and I would have solved the "bored with nothing to do" problem.

As the summer progressed, I saw a young professional in action. When Raka assumed her role as the president of the teen division of my company, she was ready to hire her first team members. Initially she picked four of her best friends, and I was relieved, but then Raka the president took over. She had a detailed discussion with me on what skills she needed in her team. The next morning she came to me with a new list. Each of the four members on her list had specific skills that Raka was comfortable with. When I asked her why she did this, her answer was simple: "If I do not have the best team, I have to do more work myself." Hmm, human resources-leadership insight.

For the roll-out meeting, Raka and I were supposed to present to the four team members and their parents. That afternoon, I was ready. My business partner Clint, as always, was assisting me to make this event a success. A few hours before the meeting, Raka was acting strangely goofy. I tried to calm her down, but it was to no avail. Finally I had to do the unthinkable. I asked her to meet me in my home office. I told her that this was a very big evening for her and me. She must calm down and seize the opportunity. A speech followed that would make any CEO managing a new president proud, but Raka looked at me and said, "Dad, please do not be mean. This is a big day for me, and I am really nervous, but don't worry. I will do all right." Amazing confidence.

When the presentation started, Raka was at her dynamic best. I did the formal introduction on the legalities of this work venture. After that, it was Raka taking over the team and explaining to them what they would do and how much money they would make. Amazing. The team was formed, a leader was born, and I found a new reason to be proud of Raka.

The team worked on four projects, all of which were for national players in the restaurant industry. The first few days the team was naturally a bit overwhelmed. They had many new things to get used to. There was me, Raka's dad, giving lectures on marketing, marketing research, project management, and other areas, there were guest speakers who are coming in to talk about public relations and media planning, and in between there were free meals at Chipotle and Quiznos. At the end of the summer each of the team members would make $400 guaranteed. Not a bad proposition.

Since this was the first job for all the teens, they did not know what to expect. There were some distracted moments, and there were moments when each was trying to go in her own direction, and we had only eight weeks. In eight weeks, the team had to research four brands and then do ad concepts and presentations on each of the brands. I was getting worried and started to doubt if this team would ever get serious about reaching its goal.

After the first week, I talked to my president, Raka, about my concern. This was one of the many moments when I started a serious discussion with her, and she made it easy by accepting the problem. No effort was spent in arguing about whether the problem existed. Instead, we were working on solutions. Raka was asking for help. She wanted to solve the problem herself. In the past, in my corporate days, I implemented a start-stop-continue process for team members. I felt that was a simple yet effective way of helping team members know what they should start doing, stop doing, and continue doing, instead of doing a too-detailed performance approval. I explained the process to Raka so that she could implement it with her team. She listened and nodded, and then she was off to bed. The CEO-president relationship changed to father-daughter. A little later I walked into her bedroom to give her a goodnight kiss. She was half asleep, staring at an episode of *Friends* on TV. I watched as I pulled the door closed behind me. There was my little president. Was this real or was I dreaming? I got to work with my princess? I was the luckiest person alive.

The next morning, there was a little extra activity before the team work session. Raka and her HR person had written down a start-stop-continue for each team member. It was done in confidence in a set of one-on-one meetings. I have done these in the past in the corporate world, but this time it was different. There was instant magic in the air. Each team member was energized and completely focused on the tasks at hand. Simply astounding.

~ If you take people seriously, not only will they be serious, but they will also teach you a thing or two. ~

1:45 AM
DENVER, COLORADO, 2007

As the teen project progressed, Clint told me about the long hours the team was putting in. I had not taken it seriously until one Saturday night that changed it all. It was 9:30 PM on a Saturday evening, and I was quickly checking my e-mail before I went down to the basement to watch a movie. Just before I was going to turn my e-mail off, a message from one of the team members popped up. She had sent me a sample ad and wanted feedback. Not only did she send me the storyboard, but she also sent me a few renderings of the actual ad. Another true first in my professional life. No agency had gone this far to show me a work in progress.

I was impressed. I realized that an effort this detailed deserved a detailed response from me. I called my brother in India who produces ad films in Mumbai. With his help, I developed a detailed list of suggestions and action steps. Then, at 10:30 PM, I forwarded all that in an e-mail to the team member.

As I watched the movie in the basement, I was still thinking about the dedication and the commitment demonstrated by this young team. When the movie finished at 1:00 AM, I went to the kitchen and emptied the dishwasher. Slowly and steadily, I was getting ready to head up to bed. My final stop was at my laptop to quickly check my e-mail.

When I opened my e-mail, there was another message from the

teen team member. To my utter astonishment, the member had used my suggestions to change the storyboard. I stared blankly at my computer screen. Wow! I was now thoroughly overwhelmed. In the middle of this overwhelming feeling, another e-mail opened on my screen. It was now 1:45 AM. This new e-mail was also from the teen team member, this time with new renderings of the ad based on the changed storyboard. The work was exactly what I desired. Perfect.

That night, I went to sleep with a major smile on my face. I knew over time each of these magic teens would shine in their chosen fields. I would then be happy to have shared their first moments of glory with them.

~ It is never too late to learn, and no teacher is too young to teach.
~

THE TEAM'S OFF-SITE DAY
DENVER, COLORADO, 2007

One afternoon the teen team was planning their day off.

They wanted to meet at the home of one of the team members instead of meeting at my place. Raka told me not to pick her up till she called me. It was four o'clock in the afternoon when I got the call and drove down to get her. There she was, with her big smile and famous first words, "Hi, Daddy." She had paint all over her face and hands, and she was carefully carrying some clothes that looked different. When I got a better look, I realized I needed an explanation.

Raka explained to me that they were spray painting and designing their own clothes. They took old clothes and created new fashion statements. The whole team of five was excited. Some of the clothes did not look that old too me, but seeing the glitter in her eyes, I decided to be the dad and not start that discussion.

Again, I started thinking of my corporate days. We had done golf outings, paintball, ropes, and other team-building exercises. But none were as professionally intimate, as creative, as spontaneous, and as easy for all involved to participate in as this. Truly something to admire.

~ Life is simple till we decide to complicate it. ~

AN EVOLVING ROLE OF A PRESIDENT
DENVER, COLORADO, 2007

In most corporate teams I have managed, the leaders have a certain element of ruthless autocratic endeavor. The leaders are focused on crossing the finish line, and if there are a few casualties in the team, the leaders view those as sacrifices that must be made in the name of the bigger picture.

Raka, as a president, was determined and focused, but she never got too assertive in showing her team that she was the president. She would not try to exert her authority on the team. She would not send e-mails to the whole group, directing them or setting expectations. Instead she would work through instant messages and text messages. She would never lose her calm. She would work with each team member.

Her style was unfamiliar to me, but I could not complain, since every deliverable was met every time. Simply stunning. Finally one day I asked her why she was not more forceful. In asking, I was implying that being forceful is a good thing and not being forceful is a bad thing.

She looked at me and said, "Dad, I cannot be the boss. After this is over, we go back to school, and we all have to be friends. Also, we are doing well, working together, and having fun. I do not want to be a jerk and ruin it for everyone."

Raka's reply made a whole lot of sense and changed my paradigm completely. What did not make sense was why I did not think of it.

~ Being unpresidential is another way to be a president. ~

BEING FAMOUS
DENVER, COLORADO, 2007

As the teen division progressed, I got a call from Kate MacArthur of *Advertising Age*. She called to ask about the teen division. As I explained it to her in detail, Kate informed me that she wanted to nominate Raka for *Advertising Age* magazine's "40 Under 40" list. Every year, *Advertising Age* magazine selects forty outstanding executives under the age of forty to recognize. It is one of the most prestigious lists to be on. I call it the executive's hall of fame. It was an "Oh My God" moment. Wow! Simply wow. Was this real? An external recognition of this magnitude meant that Raka and her team were really up to something.

A few days later when Kate called and informed me that her team had selected Raka for the list, I was totally blown away. Was it real? Raka was only thirteen years old. Another wow-moment.

What followed was a phone interview for Raka with Kate. Kate scheduled the interview, and the night before, I made a list of questions and possible answers for Raka. I sent it to her and was expecting Raka to do a few mock runs with me. Instead, she mentioned that she was tired and went to sleep.

The next day the call started, and it was a different Raka on the line. She was determined. She was direct. She was to the point. Some of her answers were completely outstanding. I was privileged to be on the phone during the interview, and, not wanting to forget a minute of their brief conversation, I furiously took down notes as the two spoke.

Kate: *What made you decide on this?*
Raka: *I have always been inspired by my dad. I have worked with him over the years. This time, I wanted to do something on my own. I love marketing.*
Kate: *Are you getting paid?*
Raka: *Yes, we are. But that is only after we complete our work and the client is happy.*
Kate: *I hear all of you are getting paid the same. Don't you think you should get paid more because you are the president?*
Raka: *Not really. In my team, every role is equally important so we all get paid the same. Yes, the company may give each one of us bonuses based on our individual work.*
Kate: *So what is it like to work with your dad?*
Raka: *It is good. I like working with him. I can challenge him if I want to, but I am respectful.*
Kate: *It was my pleasure interviewing you. You are a delightful, articulate, and talented young lady. I wish you the very best.*
Raka: *Thank you.*

~ Public relationship is all heart. Any relationship is all heart. It cannot be taught, but it can be felt. ~

July 16, 2007

Advertising Age.

40 UNDER FORTY

RAKA SEN

13

RESTAURANT MARKETING GROUP

Actually, she's 13 and three-quarters. But already Raka Sen has been working with her father, Arjun Sen, at his Restaurant Marketing Group for years as director of special analysis. This summer, she hung her shingle as president of the consultancy's newly formed teen division. After graduating from eighth grade, Ms. Sen is overseeing four peers to conduct projects for six clients, including Boston Market, Chipotle, California Pizza Kitchen and Applebee's.

"Arjun has made her a partner in his company," says Jim Adams, Chipotle's director of marketing, when asked whether Ms. Sen is a legitimate marketer. "She's delightful and bright."

Already Ms. Sen is shaping up to be an innovative boss.

"Instead of picking my friends, I picked really good workers who had things we needed," she says.

So will Ms. Sen follow in her dad's footsteps? Not precisely. "I want to go to NYU fashion-design school," she says, "and eventually market my own designs."

-- Kate MacArthur

A HUMAN RESOURCES INCIDENT DENVER, COLORADO, 2007

Every company has its unpleasant HR moments. One of the teen team members had missed work for nearly two weeks because of a family trip, and when she returned, the rest of the team had made huge progress during her absence. She found it tough to find her role in the team. Instead of saying that, she began to act up. Her attitude was simply disruptive.

First, I discussed the situation with Raka. Then I had Raka ratify my planned course of action. Next I invited the team member to my office with Clint sitting in. I explained to the team member that I was extremely disappointed in her disruptive behavior and that I had high expectations from her and held her to the highest level of performance. She listened, and then she left the room without a word.

What would happen in the corporate world? If you got reprimanded by your boss, you would go out and tell everyone how mean your boss was and how evil it was for him to be on your case. In this case, it was a completely different reaction. The team member walked down to the rest of the team members and explained to them that I came down hard on her for her behavior. She apologized to the team for being disruptive, and then she requested the team to call her out before her behavior got that far out of hand again.

I think it is a fantasy of most HR professionals to have this sort of outcome. In my case, I was fortunate to live it. What happened at the end of the work year was even more impressive. The team of five came to my office and sat around the table. They had done a performance evaluation. I was relieved to learn that the evaluation was not about me, as by now I knew the team well enough to realize that their honest, direct talk could be tough to digest at times. The team thanked me for giving them a chance to do this work, and then they shared with me the results of their performance appraisal. Of the five team members, two were recommended to get bonuses. It was also recommended that they come back the next year with a raise. A third member was also recommended to return, but with no raise. The final two members were not coming back. I was startled to hear that. Here, in front of me, were two members of the team who had been voted off the island, *Survivor* style, and they were still smiling. I could not stop myself from asking them if they agreed with the decision. They said yes, that they had not done their fair share of work and that had put added pressure on the rest of the team. It was a simple and direct answer.

Later on, Raka clarified for me that those two teens were not fired. They simply were not returning.

~ No one needs to get fired. Instead of firing people, there is a better way where everyone can evolve together. ~

THE TEST
DENVER, COLORADO, 2007

After Raka and her team finished their projects, I reached out to a group of clients to see what they felt about the teen team's work. The feedback I got from them was amazing. The words and phrases in the feedback included "surpassed my wildest expectation," "told us the same things that a megaconsultant told us," "simple thoughts, but very insightful," "amazing presentation skills," and "wow, they woke me up."

Initially, like most proud dads, I was very impressed. I wanted to keep copies of those compliments close to me to cherish frequently. But then I realized this was a test. This was a test to see if I was actually free from the corporate world. I had left the corporate world but was still allowing the corporate world to judge these super kids. I laughed. I could not believe I was falling for this. I did not need any corporate validation to tell me how cool the kids were. They had already proven to themselves that they had maximized their efforts.

As I walked down to the basement and looked at the place all the teen work had happened, I could visualize everything. Raka was standing right there when she launched the company. The team used to sit right there. That was the corner where the teens would sit on the floor and work. I remember their excitement when they used the projector the first time. I remember them jumping on the food as they worked. I remember the last day when we were getting ready to leave for the presentations and one of the teens told us with her big smile, "Just have fun." That they did. I really wish Maiji were sitting next to me as I visualized the teens. She would have been proud of the team.

In the past I had remembered such cherished moments, but this time there was a difference. The difference is what mattered. This time I was in the picture. I did not have a big role in this movie, but I did share the camera with these young stars. Yes, I was there for my Raka. I was there with her.

~ When we live by external validations, we give the corporate world control over our lives. ~

WHY RUN A MARATHON? DENVER, COLORADO, 2007-2008

If I told you that I was planning to run a marathon, you would likely visualize me to be a lean, mean, running machine. As you visualize that, let me burst your bubble. I am in no health to run a half marathon, forget a full marathon, but in June 2008, I did it. To me personally, it was important to finish the marathon, but when I think back, why I did it and how I did it was the more fascinating story.

Between 2007 and 2008, I went through a myriad of surgeries. The last of them, in August 2007, was the most brutal of them all. As I lay in the hospital bed recovering from my surgery, I was more than anxious to get home. My doctors were kind and understanding of my needs and desires, but they were equally aware of my medical needs. After repeated asking, my doctor informed Raka and me that I could leave for home once I could walk and eat on my own. That was the wrong information to give to a crazy daughter and her equally crazy father. That evening, Raka showed up at the hospital in shorts and sneakers. I was still in a daze and did not ask her why she was in that outfit, but soon Raka and my nurse were colluding and I was being prepared to go for my first walk. I started staggering, holding on to my IV pole. Raka was in front of me. As we walked around the ward once, Raka had a smile on her face; I knew she was up to something. She said, "Dad, we should go to the next ward. There are some cute women there." I knew I had no choice. So I started following my fearless leader, taking baby steps.

Once we got to the next ward, I realized Raka was totally right about the women. We were in a senior-care center. Every person there was elderly and had a big smile for me, and they waved as I walked through. Thanks to Raka, I felt like a superstar.

I started thinking of Raka's first steps. She had been very excited when she came close to walking. She would hold my hands or her mother's hands and drag her feet as she tried to learn to walk. Her excitement was tough to miss. That day in the hospital, my daughter was teaching me how to walk.

Finally, I got back to my hospital room and eased back onto my bed. I was tired. Raka sat next to the hospital bed and started doing her homework. I was dozing off after my hard day's work. The last rays of the setting sun were falling on Raka's face as she was immersed deeply in her books. Her upper body was gently oscillating. The proud dad in me watched her as I dozed off.

I may have been asleep for a few hours when I heard a gentle voice. "Dad, wake up!" I guess it was my wake-up call. I am glad it was a gentle one. I opened my eyes and stared at Raka, wondering why she had woken me up. It was 8:30 PM and I could not think of a single reason why I should be awake. But Raka had a plan, and I was half anxious to hear about it.

"Dad, are you feeling okay?" Before I could answer, she went on to say, "Glad you are feeling better. Glad you are rested. Guess what I did in the last few hours?" I looked at her and did not even attempt to answer the question, and she, as predicted, did not wait for my answer. "Dad, I have found a new walking trail for you on this floor. Let's do it! It will be our marathon."

Those of you who have a precious child know that I had no choice. The nurse was summoned, and I started my first marathon wearing the hospital gown. My right hand held on to the IV pole, and my left hand was behind me, making sure my blue hospital gown actually covered me. Raka led me through the marathon.

It was a fifteen- to twenty-minute walk. To me it felt longer. When I came back from the short walk, Raka was very happy. She announced my completion of the marathon.

That night, after Raka left for home, I sat in the hospital room thinking of my princess. I felt blessed that she was in my life. I felt life was fuller than ever as I thought of her. I could see my Maiji standing in the corner of the hospital room and smiling. Raka had shown the same calm and composed Maiji-like attitude to get me through this medical journey. Then I was the one who came up with the crazy thought. "I will run a real marathon. I will finish a real marathon. Yes, Raka, to celebrate what you mean to me, I will run a full marathon. I will finish it in one year." It was a crazy resolution, but it felt good to make it.

A few days later, I left the hospital to come back home. The fresh air outside felt good. I was happy to be going home. The healing was slow, but in a few months I was on my way to "all better."

One afternoon, as I checked the mail, my eyes fell on a direct-mail piece from Team in Training by the Leukemia & Lymphoma Society. They were offering to train people for a marathon in return for my raising funds for the society. I had run a half marathon in 2000, but it had been eight years since then. I was not sure if I could run at all, but I had made a promise to myself. I thought for a while and then kept the Team in Training brochure on my desk. I was not sure.

~ In the circle of life, one does not know when time will change the helpless of yesterday into the leaders of today. ~

2008 AND BEYOND

RETURN OF A SOCCER STAR
DENVER, COLORADO, 2008

Raka was a freshman in high school. In January, as school resumed after winter break, Raka announced to me that she was going out for soccer tryouts. I was very excited for Raka, but then again, I was worried. She had not played soccer for five years. Could she make it? I did not want my little girl to get disappointed or hurt, but I did not say a word. I was just happy that soccer was back in her life.

The days leading up to tryouts were grueling. Raka worked hard on her fitness and soccer skills. I have never seen her so determined. Every day when I picked her up from soccer, she would share with me what she had accomplished that day. She was progressing rapidly, but still I was not sure if she would make it.

Then tryouts started. They lasted over three days. On the eve of the team announcements, I sat with Raka and talked to her about what she had accomplished. I was very proud of her efforts and even though it would be very nice for her to make the team, I was judging her success based on her effort itself. Raka looked at me funny and gave me a hug before she retired to her room for the night.

The next day, I was worried and anxious all day. As I worked from home, time hung heavy on my hands. I was constantly wondering what was going on in school. Finally the time came for me to go to her school to pick her up. I was there. Raka came dashing to the car. She was on cloud nine. She had made the team.

I was pleasantly surprised and very happy for Raka. I was glad that the never-give-up Raka was back as a soccer star, and I was looking forward to watching her in action.

The season began with intense practice. Raka was a changed girl when she hung out with the other soccer girls. My car would stink with all the soccer stuff, and Raka was getting into the life of soccer and burping with the soccer girls. Then one day she got her jerseys. She was number 15. That evening, there was a photo shoot at home. I was ready for lights, camera, and action. Raka obliged me as a smiling model and donned each of the different jerseys. Later that evening, I started e-mailing the pictures to friends and family all over the world, announcing the arrival of never-give-up Raka, the soccer star.

Next, the matches started. Raka always started on the bench, then halfway into the first half the coach would put her in for a few minutes. Raka's role was to play in short bursts, and she would play her heart out for those minutes. Every time she came back to the bench, she would try to see out of the corner of her eyes if I was watching. Yes, Raka, I was taking in every moment. I did not want to miss anything.

Then came time for the big match. The reason I call it a big match is because Raka played nearly the whole time. She started in the forward line, and then the coach moved her to midfield. After halftime, Raka was the goalie. Seeing her in goal reminded me of my horror day as a goalie, but I was sure that Raka was much better than I had been.

I had my camera out and was capturing every action moment of Raka. Then came the moment when time stood still. The midfielder from the other team kicked the ball toward the goal. It was a powerful, booming shot, and the ball was coming fast at Raka. Raka was ready. Her eyes were set on the ball. The ball came to her, she jumped, and then she fisted the ball over the goalpost. What a save. I looked at my digital camera and found I was fortunate to capture the exact moment of Raka fisting the ball over the goal.

That night, after I forwarded the picture to friends and family, I looked at the picture of Raka's save. I stared at it. Ever since my goalie horror day, I have seen this save in my mind over and over.

That day, Raka had made the exact save I had seen in my mind. She had made my vision a reality.

I was extremely proud of her.

~ A never-give-up attitude always works. ~

MARATHONING STEAMBOAT SPRINGS, COLORADO, 2008

The Leukemia & Lymphoma Society's brochure was on my desk. Finally, one afternoon I opened it and realized they were holding their welcome meeting that same evening. I went to the meeting more out of curiosity than anything else. As I heard about the cause and the brave struggle of the leukemia and lymphoma patients, I decided to join the group. I would run a half marathon in Steamboat Springs.

Training started the next week. It was not easy. The first day I ran one mile in fourteen minutes. That was a great time, especially since I tried to sprint the last few steps. That day, when I was icing my shins, I realized all I needed to do was 12.2 more miles and I would complete my half marathon. I laughed. There was no way I would run the full marathon.

Slowly, training became more intense. Soon I was finishing three miles. As I ran, I realized I should not embarrass myself by calling myself a runner. I was more of a jogger. It was humbling to see the speed walkers pass me. That made me appreciate my efforts.

Raka was in disbelief when she saw my intensity in training. I had seen the same disbelief in her eyes when I had woken her up and told her that I was quitting the corporate world. By now, I knew the difference between a good disbelief and a bad disbelief. This was one of the good disbeliefs, and I had pleasantly surprised her with my training.

Four weeks into my training, I decided to run a race in downtown Denver. It was a five-mile race. I huffed; I puffed. The uphill parts of the race were brutal, but all said and done, I finished. I was tired, and somehow I managed to drive back home. It was a Saturday. Usually Raka sleeps in till noon on weekends. As I came in through the doors, I was in for a surprise. The house smelled of freshly cooked food. Raka had made a breakfast buffet to celebrate my race. She had made eggs, potatoes, chicken, and toast. On top of it there were fruits, hot chocolate, coffee, cereal, and other food items. Knowing Raka, I knew there had to be a card somewhere. Yes, there it was. Behind the toast was a precious handwritten card in which she expressed how proud she was of me. I got very emotional and gave Raka a big hug. She pulled away and looked at me and said, "Eat!" I was too emotional to let her go. Then she dished out a tiny dose of reality. "Dad, you need to eat and then shower." I got the message, loud and clear. The journey to my marathon was still a long way away. I was not sure if I would ever get there. At least I was making progress, and Raka was sweet enough to celebrate my journey.

I enjoyed the breakfast buffet. I had earned it. More than the food, I realized Raka was taking me seriously as I started running. It felt good to run at a pace of a thirteen-minute mile and be taken seriously. My pace was no accomplishment—I was one of the slowest finishers in my age group—but at least I was running and Raka was celebrating just that. I finished my breakfast and was clearing the table when I realized I had made up my mind to run the half marathon in Steamboat Springs.

The next few weeks of training were tough as I started feeling different kinds of pain and injuries. Visits to physical therapists became more frequent than running. I would think back about the days after I quit the corporate world. The pain that came from the training for the marathon was similar to the pain I experienced from the days I was home and not doing anything. Those days I was tempted to accept a corporate job and end the pain of loneliness. During my marathon, I was tempted to stop training and end my pain and misery. But somehow, I decided to go on, as Raka was looking forward to my running.

Two weeks before the race was the last long run. I was excited and on that day I ran sixteen miles. I have to confess, I was hurting a lot after that effort, but that gave me the confidence I needed for my half marathon. As I drove back from practice, a strange thought came to my mind. I just ran *more* than half a marathon. That means I was closer to a marathon. Wow, that was a scary thought.

The next day, between work and icing my feet, I had a crazy idea. Could I finish a full marathon? "No way," I told myself, but I was not done thinking about the issue. I thought about it all day.

That evening over dinner I did the unthinkable. I told Raka that I was thinking of running the full marathon. It was funny, seeking her permission and trying to reach out for her wisdom. It is amazing to think how life changes. Not too long ago, she was seeking permission from me.

Raka was watching TV. Her eyes were still on the TV when she told me, "Dad, if you think you can, you should do it." Hmm. What did she mean? Was she okay with me running a full marathon? I did not know.

The next morning, I woke up and changed my race to a full marathon. I am never scared or nervous about anything, but this was an exception, as I was extremely nervous. Two days before the race, Raka and I got to Steamboat Springs. The day before the race, we just hung out without any plan. After lunch, we found a pottery store. We each did a piece to commemorate the occasion. Then Raka and I decided to drive the race route. The last time I had decided to look ahead before a journey was when I had looked at my life's path after the wake-up call on the day after 9/11. That was the day I saw what lay ahead and how I would regret it if I followed the corporate path. But seeing the path ahead helped me change my direction. This time, driving the race path was extremely important because I needed to plan my run.

I was very tense as we drove. I made a note of every small uphill and downhill area of the route. When it took us close to forty minutes to drive the hilly course, I was very worried.

When we reached the starting point, close to ten thousand feet above sea level, Raka took over. I had not realized that she had been paying such detailed attention to the course as we drove. She started, "Dad, this is easy. First you run for three miles and come to the three buffalos. They are sitting on the right side. They look very lazy and most probably will not move between now and tomorrow. Then at mile six is the bridge of hope. Once you cross the bridge, you get closer to mile seven. But be careful at mile eight. Do not look left. Do not look, Dad, okay?" I was startled and asked myself, "What is she talking about? Why should I not look left? Hmm!" But Raka was on a roll. She pointed left and showed me what I should be avoiding. There was a scarecrow staring at us. "Dad, be careful of this scarecrow."

As we continued to drive back, Raka constantly broke down the race course for me. I simply nodded my head, listening to all the wisdom coming from my little princess. I was getting overwhelmed with this when Raka got a phone call. She picked up the phone and started talking to whoever called her. I heard her say, "Guess what! I just finished a marathon! I did it in thirty minutes." Of course she was talking about our driving 26.2 miles in thirty minutes. I chuckled in my mind and had to say, "Very funny, Raka!"

The night before the marathon was one of the longest nights in my life. We had the pasta dinner with other racers and then Raka and I hit our beds by 9:00 PM. I had read about pre-marathon jitters. It was true. I closed my eyes but was wide awake. It was evident that Raka, too, was wide awake. Finally, after thirty minutes (though to me it felt like hours) of pretending to be asleep, Raka asked me, "Dad, are you awake?"

"Yes, baby," I said. She got out of her bed and came and sat next to me.

"Dad, I have to ask you something. Do you want to run tomorrow?"

I did not understand what she was saying. I looked blankly at her. I also looked at the time. In five hours I needed to be in the lobby of the hotel. What was Raka talking about, me not running the next day? It was not making sense.

Raka held my hands and said, "Dad, you do not have to run tomorrow. I am scared. I did not realize a marathon is this long. It is OK with me if you do not run. I love you, Dad. You are my hero even if you do not run tomorrow." It was incredible to see that Raka was feeling responsible. I learned that children, when they are ready, need to be given responsibility. As they receive responsibility, they start acting with responsibility.

I smiled at her and realized how deeply she cared about me. I gave her a big hug and knew this was a moment that would define us in the future. I had to say something smart. I had to assure her that everything would be fine.

"Raka—" I paused. "I love you, baby. I know you are worried, but remember I have been training for four months for this day. I have put myself in the position, and I owe it to myself to try. If I try, I can succeed. But if I do not try, I will fail." I realized that many times in life, people stop trying because they do not believe they can succeed. And once they stop trying, they eliminate any chance of success. Hence, trying was the key.

Raka was not at all convinced with my answer. She held my hand tightly. I realized that my baby was scared. I pulled her close and promised her everything would be fine. I would finish and would be in good health. I promised.

Raka was not convinced. It was close to 1:00 AM when we finally negotiated a solution. Raka would wait for me at the 23.5-mile marker. Once I got there, she would run with me to the finish line. I was happy to agree to this. After that, she went to her bed, and very soon I heard soft, mild breathing. She was fast asleep.

I rested a little and then it was time to get ready for the race. I was scared as I walked down to the hotel lobby. A bus took some of us to the starting point. It was chilly, and as I stood at the starting line, I was hit by the same fear that had hit Raka the night before. I was sure this was a very bad idea. I tried to rationalize with myself that I had worked hard to put myself in this position. It did not work. Then I saw light. In 23.5 miles, or four and half hours, I would see Raka. That thought lit up my face, and I was ready to start the race.

As I started running, my first lookout was for the three buffaloes. I got to them in forty minutes. Raka was right. They were there, waiting for me. I gave them a thankful glance and started toward the bridge of hope. Anytime I would I see anyone next to the course, I would give them Raka's cell number to call. Raka was getting updates from strangers who were telling her that her dad has crossed the mile three marker. I am sure she was happy to get a live report on my running.

As I crossed the bridge of hope, I had my hands raised, as I was proud. Next would be the scarecrow on the left, but I would be sure not to look at it, lest it jinx me. Close to eight miles, I realized I was passing the scarecrow. I dashed past it then came to the breeze point. That was the point where I would come down one hill and start climbing the next hill. There would be a clean breeze to freshen me up. Once I reached that point, I raised my arms to enjoy nature's spa. I was refreshed.

I crossed the halfway point in two and a half hours. I was on target. I knew in another two hours I would see my baby. I knew she was waiting for me anxiously.

I was getting tired. The sun was getting to me. My legs were tired, but I felt I could do it. Mile fifteen came a few minutes after three hours. I was at the baby-step area, a long uphill zone. The hill was getting to me. I felt like slowing down and walking a little, but I could not stop as I did not want to delay my meeting Raka. I decided to run on. I decided to run to her, and then I would walk with her, if needed.

Mile twenty finally came. I had slowed down, a lot. I didn't realize at what point my heart took over. Even though I was slowing down, I was gliding forward slowly but surely. I was focused. I realized that it would be less than an hour before I would see her. I could not wait.

My effort was more intense as I crossed the twenty-two-mile marker. It was pure willpower now. I was confident I would reach Raka. After 22.7 miles, I got excited about seeing my baby. I was so proud to have come this far. I was also sure that Raka would get me to finish the race. I did not have to wait for too long. Raka was getting restless waiting for me at mile 23.5 and decided to run back to meet me. Our meeting at the twenty-three-mile marker was memorable. We ran into each other and gave each other a tight hug. I was in tears and was overflowing with emotions. Raka very soon got over her emotions and was in a tactical mode. "Dad, we still have more than three miles to go. We cannot wait here for too long. Do you want water? Do you need any Gatorade?" She had all the supplies for me in her backpack. I was ready to let her lead me. We held hands and started walking briskly to the finish line.

It was not easy. We still had a way to go. It was getting tougher and was starting to hurt a lot, but Raka was in no mood to give up. She was determined to do her part to get me across the finish line. I was relieved that she was in charge.

Soon we passed the pottery place where we had painted the day before. I paused to look at the place. Raka was in no mood to contemplate. She was focused. I felt a pull and realized that I had to move on. Slowly, we walked into the downtown area of Steamboat Springs. I could feel the end was near. As Raka walked next to me, holding my hand, I was reminded of the beginning of this marathon. The marathon had not started that morning. For me, it had started in the hospital room, where Raka had held my hand and got me to do one lap around the hospital ward. We were very close to finishing this long journey. I held Raka's hand tightly.

Just as I held Raka's hand tightly, she left my side and went over to the pavement. I was startled but did not have the energy to follow her. Then I realized that the finish line was just ahead. She wanted me to enjoy my moment by myself. I saw cameras flashing. I tried to put a smile on my face as I crossed the finish line. The wet towel felt good, but, more than anything, I was proud to hold my medal. I did not have the energy to scream, but deep inside I was screaming, "Raka, we did it. Yes, we did. Thank you!" My mind went back to my frail body in the hospital room and Raka dragging me out to walk around the ward. From there, we had come a long way. I had actually finished a marathon. And I had done that with Raka. What a day.

As I sat down to rest, Raka was on the phone calling friends and family. She was so proud of my accomplishment. You could sense her pride as she told others about my finishing. This reminded me of my telling everyone about Raka's story. Isn't it tough to visualize how fast our children grow up and are ready to take over the reign of our lives?

~ The smallest of steps is the first step to a
life-changing marathon. ~

FIVE MORE COOKIES
DENVER, COLORADO, 2008

Every semester, before Raka's final examinations, she gets frantic with last-minute studying. One year, I started the tradition of baking a big good-luck cookie for her to ease her stress. I do not know exactly when we started the tradition, but it has become a ritual for us.

I think back to my school days and my final examinations. Every few hours, Maiji was always there with food and refreshments. She would get me fresh fruits, nuts, hot chocolate, or some homemade yogurt. When brought the food to my study desk and stood next to me, I felt important, I felt special. I wish Maiji were around for Raka during her final examinations.

Every semester, Raka had to feel that it was the most special cookie of all. As the cookie tradition became big for Raka and me, I would plan for months. I would get new recipes from my interns and was always looking for some new ingredients to use in the next recipe.

In January 2008, Raka was getting ready for her final examinations, and I was in the kitchen getting ready to bake her a pecan-almond chocolate chip cookie. First I hand-sliced the pecans and almonds very thin. Then I prepared the dough. After the dough was ready, I gently added the Ghirardelli chocolate chips. The chocolate chips were stirred in but had to remain whole. Raka loved it when the chocolate chips baked whole and exploded inside a cookie. After baking the cookie for exactly twelve minutes, I reached in to get it out of the oven.

As the hot cookie lay in front of me on the kitchen counter, a thought dawned on me; after this there would be only five more cookies. That's it. Raka would have one more set of finals her sophomore year, two more sets of finals her junior year, and two more sets her senior year. That gave me only five more chances.

There was something about that information that overwhelmed me emotionally. I could see time rushing away and my days of baking cookies for her finals gone. I stared at the cookie. I wanted to grab the cookie in my arms and hold it close to me. I was in tears. I did not know if the tears came from realizing how fortunate I was to have Raka in my life or the few days ahead before she left for college.

There I was, a forty-three-year-old man standing in the kitchen, reflecting on the main criterion for in my life. Was it money in the bank? Nah, I came to this country with $320 and was happy even through days when I made only $5000 a year. Was it the size of my house? Was it my health? Finally I asked myself the right question. What one thing could I not afford to lose in life? What one thing was most scarce in my life? What one thing, even if I tried, could I not get more of? The answer was very clear: time with Raka.

Based on my divorce settlement, Raka is with me half of the time. That gives me every other weekend and every Wednesday and Thursday. Wednesdays and Thursdays are busy days with homework and music lessons, so weekends are the only time I can really bond with Raka. In April 2007, I put all the dates on a spreadsheet and lo and behold, I realized I had only 115 weekends left with my daughter before she left for college. In fact, right after she turned fourteen in October 2007, the number would go below one hundred.

I was sad that it had taken me so long to realize this, but it also felt good to know how little time I had so I could enjoy every weekend with her. Right away, I started planning our time together. I wanted to get the maximum out of every minute with Raka.

The math in my spreadsheet is simple, but the facts are stunning. If you are a new parent I will leave you with one number. You have

6,570 days before your child is eighteen and leaves for college. (The actual number is 6,574 if you adjust it for leap years.)

Now I was counting weekends with Raka, and I was counting the number of cookies left before graduation. I was thinking about all this as I took the cookie to Raka. She was deep in her studies and looked up at me as I walked in with the cookie. I wanted to give her a tight hug. I just put the cookie next to her and stood there for a few minutes. I was thinking of the way Maiji stood next to me. Raka went back to studying, and from time to time she would reach out and grab a bite of the cookie. I finally backed out of the room. As I left, I looked at Raka one last time. "My baby!" I said to myself.

~ We all have miracles bestowed upon us. All we need to do is wake up and reach out for them. ~

READING BETWEEN THE LINES DENVER, COLORADO, 2008

The summer of 2008 did not start very well for Raka.

The semester leading to the summer break was rocky. Her grades were fluctuating, and Raka was not settled. Boys were everywhere, but more than boys, she was not very sure about who she wanted to be friends with. Raka's mom and I felt that a change was needed. We felt Raka needed to go to a different school. Maybe a private school would fix things.

Now when I think back, I am not sure that private school was the right answer, but we were convinced that any change would be better than no change at all.

So the search for the perfect private school began. We shortlisted two schools—one was an all-girls school, and the other was co-ed. Raka was strongly opposed to any change, as she felt the change would be a disaster. Even through her refusal, she left the door open for me to at least try a little.

First we set up some rules. The rules were simple. Raka had to cooperate and I would, in return, cooperate back with Raka by including her in the decision process. Raka's cooperation included two things, participating in the school visits and then filling out the application forms. Raka was not fully happy with this setup. She wanted to increase her odds by including my brother, Oni, in the decision process. I was tired of fighting with Raka and agreed that

Oni could have the deciding vote. I also promised to play it fair by not calling Oni or trying to influence him.

Even though Oni was the final tiebreaker, Raka felt good about her chances with Oni and right away approached him. A long e-mail from Raka reached my brother. Raka was very confident that her favorite Oni Kaka would decide in her favor.

The reply from Oni surprised even me. Oni had done a lot of personal soul searching and reflected back on his growing-up days and how his poor academic records nearly closed all doors in life. He had sided with the parents. I could not believe it. Raka was shocked and accused me of influencing my brother, but I knew that I was clean.

After that, Raka had to join me for two visits to the schools. The all-girls school was first. Raka and I showed up at the school and were greeted by the principal. The principal looked at Raka's face and realized that Raka was here against her wishes. One of the current students came in to take Raka for a tour of the school. While Raka was out on tour, I spoke to the principal.

The tour did not last too long, and when she returned, I thanked the principal, and Raka and I walked back to the car. I was going down memory lane, thinking of my Jesuit high school in Kolkata, India, St. Lawrence High School. This school was just like St. Lawrence. Raka would be perfect here.

But as we walked to the car, Raka needed no urging to tell me that this school would not work. "Dad, they barely have a soccer team." Raka went on to describe everything that was lacking in the school. I drove home and listened to her, and I sensed fear and nervousness in her voice. I realized she was scared of the change. I realized for the first time that this was a big change and the results were not guaranteed.

I also remembered the promise I had made Raka during my divorce from her mom. I had promised Raka that I would do my best to make sure she went to the same middle school and high school, as I wanted her to make friends. Of course this change would uproot her and she would have to start making new friends all over again. I remembered a professional colleague of mine who had once mentioned that children are very robust and can very easily adapt to new situations. How could this colleague be wrong? After all, he was extremely successful professionally and had moved his family every two years all over the world as he moved up the corporate ladder. I also felt that this could be one of the situations where Raka's ability to make new friends was not as important as the big picture.

I was driving home with my mind still back at the school we had just visited. Raka was listening to some music on her iPod. We both were in our own worlds, when Raka broke the silence.

"Dad, you know if you send me to this all-girl school, I will definitely turn gay." I was startled by her way of thinking. I just looked at her and nodded my head. I wanted to say, "Baby, I am okay with that," but then when I saw the expression in her face, I realized this was no light moment. She was shaken up. She was *very* scared of the change.

I reached out and held her hand. She looked at me. I asked her, "Baby, do you trust me?"

She did not hesitate before stating, "Yes, Dad."

"Then do not worry such a lot. I will make sure that the best thing happens to you," I said. But as I said it I was not sure about the change of school. I decided not to share my doubts with her but to keep them to myself.

A few days later, we visited the second school. This time Raka was in a different mood. She was strong and confident. At the school, Raka was engaged in the discussion and asked questions. Her questions were not easy. I guess she was taking the direct-attack approach.

When we returned home, Raka was supposed to write an essay for her application, saying why she was excited about joining the school. She was a little hesitant when I reminded her of her promise, but she sat down with the laptop. After a few hours of work, Raka was ready to show me what she had written. I was ready to read a breakthrough essay. Raka is gifted as a writer. When I reviewed the document, I realized that it was, at most, one hundred words long. Raka had poured her heart out, and in the process the reader would have no doubt about where she stood on the issue. Raka was completely against the idea of a change.

I realized that the document would kill any chance she had of making the school. I tried to explain to her that she must make a more convincing case for her application. Raka listened to me and went back to her laptop. A few minutes later, she came back and said, "Dad, you realize that you are asking me to lie to get into this school. Don't you think the school does not want me to lie?" *That is a good point,* I thought. I was thinking of a way to overcome this objection when Raka struck again. "Dad, based on our agreement, I am only supposed to write and fill out the application forms. I am not required to lie to get in."

Hmm, now this is tough, I thought.

That night when I went to bed, I read Raka's letter again. Even though the words were cleverly chosen and Raka was able to communicate the subliminal message of not being interested, I read between the words. There was a little girl who was scared. She was scared of changes. She had heard stories about private schools and was worried. She was also worried about leaving her friends behind. Her fears were very genuine.

I realized that Raka's mom and I were in a losing battle. Instead of letting the battle trickle down to a total loss for us, I offered Raka a contract. The contract was a way out. We clearly wrote down what we expected from Raka. We also defined what rewards Raka would get once she accomplished her goals. If Raka failed to reach the goals, she had to go through a school transfer.

Raka read the entire contract. Then she looked at me and asked, "So you are not sending me to private school?"

I replied, "Not now." I tried to explain the contract in detail, but Raka was done listening. She grabbed the contract and signed immediately. She felt she had accomplished her goal. She was relieved.

She came to me and gave a big hug. She was happy.

~ Is change for the sake of change, without knowing the results, worth it? ~

CABARET NIGHT
DENVER, COLORADO, 2009

I grew up in an environment where conforming was key, and adults with limited knowledge determined our future potential. Let me be honest. Instead of determining future potential, some adults closed some doors for us, forever. I have already shared with you my story of the death of a painter, when I stopped any association with painting when I was eleven.

So now you can imagine my reaction when Raka came to me and said that she would audition for a solo in the school's annual musical performance, *The Cabaret*. I knew Raka was taking lessons from her music teacher. Her teacher is inspiring, and Raka was making steady progress, but with my zero music knowledge, there was no way to judge how good Raka was. As neither Raka's mom nor I were any good in music, I never saw Raka as a movie star. I was just happy that Raka enjoyed music and was taking it seriously. Was she ready to audition for a solo? I was not sure.

Raka practiced hard. Sometimes I sneaked up the staircase and sat at the top of the stairs to listen to her practice. I would close my eyes and listen to my baby sing her heart out. I did not know how good she was, but I could feel that she was enjoying her music.

Then came the evening of her performance. Raka got special tickets for me, and I sat on one side of the stage while the kids performed on the other side of the stage. The auditorium was nearly full. The performance started with a few solos. The kids were good, and I was worried about Raka. Could she stand tall among these good singers? Raka's turn came. She was a little nervous, but she started with confidence. Soon she was in a groove, and I listened to her in total astonishment. I was completely enchanted. This was my daughter. She was singing a solo in front of a live audience. Wow!

There was a small hesitation in the second half of her solo, but she finished strong, and her friends in the audience greeted her with loud applause. She had done it.

I am so glad she did not read my mind when I judged her singing skills. If she had listened to me, she may not have sung for another twenty-two years. I was proud that I'd kept quiet and not interrupted her journey to the top of the world.

~ If you are determined, there is no trying and failing. ~

WOW 1 MORE™

Recently I started a keynote speech in which I talk about the concept of "Wow 1 More." I explain the concept by showing that when you go to Starbucks to buy a cup of coffee, you are going to *one* Starbucks, *one* time, to buy *one* cup of coffee from *one* person at Starbucks. The problem arises, and service standards drop, if the Starbucks order-taker sees you as one of many customers who will come to the store that day and, as a result, dishes out a not-so-special service.

As consultants, many times we talk the talk but don't walk the talk. We are notorious for living by the rule, "Do what I say, not what I do."

On a Saturday morning, I was getting ready to go out to golf with my friends. Raka was sleeping. Normally I leave her instructions to make her own breakfast and wait for me to return. That morning, as I was having my breakfast, the concept of "Wow 1 More" hit me. I realized that I have my own restaurant, and in my restaurant, I have one customer. I get a chance to wow her every morning when I make breakfast for her, every day when she comes home from school, and during the weekends when she is with me. This thought was very closely connected to my realization about the five more cookies.

The moment I realized this, it changed my actions. In consulting, we talk about information that makes action inevitable. This was one of those pieces of information. That day, instead of leaving her a note, I decided to bake some fresh pastries for Raka. The next morning's breakfast, before she went to school, was special. The school lunch she took was in a red paper bag, not the regular brown bag. I also preprinted stickers with custom messages to seal the bag. That day's sticker said, "Raka is cool." The following Tuesday when I picked Raka up and drove her to her music lessons, I had a homemade salmon burger on a plate with a Starbucks latte. I was proud that finally I realized what "Wow 1 More" actually meant in my life.

~ Let us roll out the white tablecloth for
those who matter the most. ~

HIBERNATE

Now let us get back to "hibernate." I remember the days and months Raka would prompt me to ask her to spell the word *hibernate*. That was a very important word in Raka's life. It was the first multisyllable word she learned to spell.

We spent numerous hours in a car or at home when she would say, "ask me to spell *hibernate*." Before I could ask her the question, she would start, "H-I-B-E-R-N-A-T-E." Amazing.

Now when I think back, I do not think it is a coincidence that she was spelling *hibernate*. I think she was giving me a signal. I think she was trying to tell me, "Wake up, Dad, before life passes you by." Otherwise, why did she choose the word *hibernate*?

For a long time, I failed to get it. I get it now, Raka. Yes, I do, and I am awake. Wink!

~ The message is loud and clear. Messengers can come in different shapes and sizes, but are we ready to get the message? ~

EPILOGUE

Initially I named this book *Raising a Daughter.* As I wrote it, I realized who was raising whom. It was the dad who needed to be raised. So the change in name was a no-brainer. It was my education of a lifetime.

My intent in writing this book was simple. I wanted to give it to Raka as her Christmas gift. I wanted to tell her about her goodness. But the book turned out to be my own gift because I enjoyed reliving those moments as I wrote. As I wrote, I cried, I smiled, and I lived through many different emotions. I revisited my life experiences from today's reality. Sometimes reliving the moments taught me things I had missed learning the first time. I really did not want this book to end.

When I look at the days before I woke up, I am startled. What was I thinking? How could I have been so confused? My reality back then was different. As I go back and forth between the two realities, I have to confess that I like today's reality better and would like to hold on to it. The past reality had more excitement. It was full of uncertainty. I was never in control and was always striving to get ahead. Every time I won, I celebrated. But I did not notice that every time I won, someone else lost.

Life for me has changed. Whereas before I was a high-risk player willing to travel thousands of miles in search of a change, today's reality is more mundane and routine. Raka and I do nearly the same things every week. Our weekends have no big parties. We are home. We cook together, and then we watch a movie. Sometimes we reward ourselves by going to bed early. Why is today's reality, being somewhat boring, still way better than the past? Why am I happier? The answer is very simple. In today's reality, I have my Raka. And I have myself.

Raka has turned me into a better person. I am more patient with people, and maybe a little bit more caring and compassionate. Unlike my corporate days, when I was ruthless with people, I am kinder and more patient with my team members in my consulting company. Anytime anyone in the company goofs, I remember Raka's golden words, "You should critique the act or the deed. You should not critique the person." Yes, little Raka would roll her eyes when she was in trouble and tell me, "Dad, I am not a bad person. It is my action that is bad." This was a very important lesson in the professional world because it helped me see the bigger picture and potential in people.

Finally, Raka has taught me that in life, family matters and nothing else does. Over time, I have learned to appreciate my team members' commitment to their families. It is very rewarding when my team reaches out to me in my hours of need. I have to admit, in the corporate days my team would throw me birthday parties that were bigger and better every year, but today when my team reaches out to help me they are sincere. It makes working more fun.

But how did all this happen? Did I change on my own? No. The journey started with Maiji holding my hands and guiding me when I was little. It continued with my dad choosing aeronautical engineering for my major and my university friends supporting me in my campaign for student vice president. Next came Professor Heike at Brigham Young University, whose belief in me startled me but helped me choose my profession. All these people were just laying the groundwork that got me ready to open my eyes and experience the miracle that came on September 15, 1993, in the form of a tiny baby named Raka. Raka took me through baby steps and then bigger steps to advance to a better life. I salute my little teacher.

It has been a lot of learning so far, but I am not done yet. I still have two more years of daily classes, and I am looking forward to every lesson.